Lorelei Vashti

DRESS, MEMORY

A memoir of my twenties in dresses

ALLEN&UNWIN
SYDNEY • MELBOURNE • AUCKLAND • LONDON

Author's note: This book is based on true events, but some people and events have been combined for narrative purposes. Some names have been changed to protect the anonymity of those involved. The author is of the firm belief that life writing of any kind should be prefaced by the timeless wisdom of George Bernard Shaw: 'All autobiographies are lies.'

First published in 2014

Allen & Unwin
83 Alexander Street
Crows Nest NSW 2065
Australia
Phone: (61 2) 8425 0100
Email: info@allenandunwin.com
Web: www.allenandunwin.com

Cataloguing-in-Publication details are available
from the National Library of Australia
www.trove.nla.gov.au

ISBN 978 1 74331 101 1

Internal design by Allison Colpoys
Photography by Jo Duck, www.joduck.com
Set in 12/19 pt Bodoni by Post Pre-press Group, Australia
Printed in Australia by McPherson's Printing Group

10 9 8 7 6 5 4 3 2 1

To both my families,
the vintage and the brand new.

An adventure may be worn as a muddy spot or it may be worn as a proud insignia. It is the woman wearing it who makes it the one thing or the other.

Norma Shearer

Contents

Prologue

When I was twenty my heart started beating so loudly it terrified me. I went to a doctor and she told me I was having a panic attack and that I should try to breathe either more or less, I can't remember which. Then, in a whimsical offhand way, and in a tone of voice that wasn't medical, she added that next time I was freaking out maybe I could try focusing my attention on something other than the distorted white noise of my own mind: why not try—say, for example—focusing on the hem of my dress?

That day I was wearing what my friend Beck used to call my Mintie dress—green and white—which I'd chopped off and re-hemmed myself, tacking it in a clumsy schoolgirl Home Ec way. As I sat and concentrated on the wonky stitching, I did calm down. Years later, I understand how this tactic can helpfully disembody oneself from one's addled brain, but back then neither I nor the doctor could have known that her excellent advice would encourage me to go and build an entire pharmacy full of hems over the next ten years: one which—to my great pride and absolute shame—now fills five wardrobes across two states.

I work as a freelance writer and editor, which means I hardly need to leave the house if I don't want to. Still, putting on a particular outfit can mean the difference between being able to focus on the work or sitting there, helplessly grappling with my thoughts for hours. I have tried to throw dresses out, give them away or otherwise let go of them, but whenever I do I go through such an overdramatic grieving process for a particular dress and its associated memory. The dresses stayed.

It seems obvious to state that clothing has some power over our emotions. Most of us can relate to the idea that dressing smartly for a job interview helps us feel more confident; we have all heard stories of actors preparing for a role by dressing in the clothes their character would wear. I recently read a study that discovered people score more highly on cognitive exercises when they're wearing a white lab coat—apparently the brain makes a connection between the item of clothing and the reputation doctors and scientists have for being careful and rigorous, and they take on those characteristics themselves. On the other hand, if you're told the coat belongs to a painter—a less 'intellectual' profession—you won't score any better, because the power of a piece of clothing depends on the symbolic meaning you give to it. However, I still think the best way to observe the influence clothes have over our own psychological state is to wake up every morning and just get dressed.

The popular line goes that wearing something fabulous can make you feel like a new person, but as someone who collects dresses, most mornings my goal is the opposite: I want to feel like an old person, or rather, be reminded of the old person who used to be me. Even as I move away from her towards the safer harbour of the future, these flashes of my old selves, relentless and repetitive, illuminate my way. Memory, like a lighthouse, shines the most vivid moments back to us, over and over, and these stories, often unexpectedly chosen by our memories for us to return to again and again, become the myths we stitch together and inhabit every time we try to answer the question, 'Who am I?'

In the same way that each word of a writer's story is carefully chosen to tell a particular tale, the twelve dresses that make up this book capture the most exceptional moments of many stories—of shock, betrayal and love—that altogether made up my twenties. It was a period I was expecting certain things to happen in a certain way—romance, career, intoxicating new friendships and travel to exotic places—but often it wasn't according to plan.

That Mintie dress has been re-hemmed many times over the years: only once on a sewing machine properly, by my ex-boyfriend's mum, when we visited her out in the middle of Queensland. I am still reminded of her when I wear it, as well as that first doctor in Brisbane who suspected I was tumbling into a years-long blackout before I could see it myself. The dress also makes me recall the kindness of the Qantas air hostess who offered me tissue after tissue as I wore it and wept for the entire flight on my first move to Melbourne in 2003; also, the man who skilfully disunited me from it years later in his bedroom above the New York bar where, moments earlier, we had been drinking White Russians.

Some people remember stages of their lives through the smells of certain places or the music they were listening to during that time. I remember them through my clothes. The dresses are precious because they mean something to me. Things become more valuable once you know the story behind them, and here is mine.

Once upon a time

I was named after a siren, a mythical German mermaid whose haunting beauty lured sailors to their deaths, but from early on my family teased me that my whining and wailing was more like the siren of an ambulance: loud, squealy and hyperactive. I was prone to losing my voice from over-use, always shouting to be heard above my three siblings.

The year I was born my parents built a house at the bottom of Buderim mountain, a long-extinct volcano in Queensland. The same rich soil that had encouraged banana, coffee and ginger plantations to flourish there during the late nineteenth century found its way onto the soles of our shoes and into the grazes of our knees a hundred years later. Buderim was a good place for things to grow. My parents planted a large strawberry patch on our ten acres of land and we sometimes helped pick them, pushing our carts backwards down the rows, popping more strawberries into our mouths than into the white polystyrene trays to be packed and sent to market. At the end of the season there were still so many strawberries left, turning over-ripe in the patch, that we used them as artillery in strawberry fights, flinging near-rotting fruit at each other until our old T-shirts were stained the colour of wine, and seeds stuck knottily in our hair.

Butterflies, pinned like startled first-place ribbons, clung inside frames to the walls of our house. My dad was an entomologist who always carried a net and a magnifying glass to catch and study insects. I observed them trapped in their jars filled with ethyl acetate, watching as if it was a show as their wings flittered frantically and then stopped still. But every week he would turn the lens the other way round, rehearsing and performing in one amateur musical each year, usually in the handsome leading-man roles, allowing himself to be pinned and captured under a spotlight as I watched on in fascination from the audience.

My two older sisters, Xanthe and Analiese, were born a year apart, and spent their childhoods perfecting a cute double stage act. From the beginning, they were a hit, doing dance classes together and always being cast in shows wearing identical frilly dresses with their hair crimped. One year when they were ten and eleven, they performed in a butterfly-catchers' dance, elegantly swooping their miniature toy nets on rods in matching yellow dresses made by our mum, a dressmaker who created not just the costumes for the shows my family were in but also all our everyday clothes. The butterfly-catchers' dresses were sumptuous, made out of metres of fabric. They hung heavy and limp until my sisters moved, and then they came to life. When my sisters pinched at the two bottom corners of the skirt, the folds of material fanned out and looked like butterflies' wings. When they spun around the skirts seemed to lift them up.

I wanted to act on stage too, but there didn't seem to be any role for me up there. The one person left to duet with was my brother Lachy but he was only interested in sport. So twice a week I took a sleeping bag to the old community hall where rehearsals were held, and curled up tiny as an ant on the hard wooden floorboards at the back of the room, by myself, to watch the actors rehearse. The director made them perform the scenes repeatedly, and I learnt that if you wanted to get something right you had to do it over and over again. I saw the shows so many times—*Pippin*, *Oklahoma*, *Show Boat*, *South Pacific*—that I knew all the lines, and took the words out to the strawberry patch with me after school, playing every role and pretending the thousands of little bright red berry faces were my audience.

But I longed for a proper audience. In grade six my best friend Katherine and I auditioned for a variety show and we got parts as old-time radio singers. We wore my sisters' matching yellow butterfly-catcher dresses and sang 'You're Never Fully Dressed Without a Smile' from *Annie*, harmonising in cute American accents. I looked out into the audience, the lights bright, my view reversed, feeling like I'd come to life as I gently swished the skirt in time to the music. The tiny insects were looking at *me* now. The applause rang in my ears for days.

As the years went by, the theatre rescued me again and again. It was a sanctuary from the trials and disappointments of adolescence, where I could wear make-up and dress in crazy costumes and pretend to be different people. In our final year of high school Katherine announced she was going away for a year on a student exchange. I begged my parents to let me go on one as well. I didn't want to miss out. I couldn't bear Kat doing something adventurous and fun without me. Mum and Dad said no way: they couldn't afford it. But that's when the theatre saved me again, in a roundabout way. Dad was working on a community production of *Les Misérables* when the barricade ran over his foot during a performance and sliced it open at the ankle so he couldn't walk. It was gory and agonisingly painful for him, and it would take a long time to heal. There was an up-side, though, as the local council gave him a compensation payout, which meant I was able to go on an exchange after all. It was the first time I got to do something all of my own, to go somewhere my sisters hadn't already been first, to wear all the make-up and fantastic costumes and try on a new character for real.

It was late in the year, and all the popular countries had already been taken so there were only three countries still available—all the places other teenagers didn't want to go: Iceland, Latvia and Turkey.

I talked it over with Kat at recess. I had always had a dream to live in a bohemian enclave, an artists' colony where everyone wore outlandish outfits and had after-dinner sing-alongs and painted *en plein air* in their backyards sporting natty straw hats. Kat and I listened to Björk and decided there was nowhere else in the world weirder than Iceland. I'd also seen a documentary about it on SBS, and that sealed the deal: Iceland was the most bohemian enclave of our time. 'It's so cold there that all they can do is stay inside and make art!' I told Kat.

'Make out?' Kat asked.

'Make *art*,' I said.

But when I told my parents which country I'd chosen, they vetoed it on account of my vegetarianism. I had refused to eat meat since I was four years old, when I found out during a visit to a farm (lambs frolicking in pastures, cows peacefully chewing their cud) that this was where the meat came from. It was another thing that marked me as separate from my family.

Dad had never approved. He was concerned I wasn't getting enough nutrients, and we were always having stand-offs about it at the dinner table. He considered it fussiness, a deliberate ploy to get attention, and maybe it had been at the start, but eventually it became entrenched and there was no going back. Throughout my teenage years they had both gradually accepted it, and now Mum even made me separate meat-free meals. 'Iceland is exactly the wrong place for a vegetarian,' Dad said gruffly. 'There'll be nothing for you to eat.'

'And Latvia is so meaty too,' Mum pointed out. 'All those stews! I'm afraid you'll have to go to Turkey. At least they eat vegetables there.'

'Well at least she's not vegan,' Dad reminded Mum. Even though we didn't personally know any vegans at that time, they were both always fearful I might go the extra step.

Although I had to shake off my attachment to Iceland, I soon found myself excited by the idea of spending a year in Turkey. I loved history, and Turkey was steeped in it. Besides, who ever went to Turkey? When I told people at school they asked me if I would have to wear a burqa, and I rolled my eyes and told them of course not, but secretly I didn't know. Turkey was exotic and intriguing, and the more I learnt about it in the lead-up to going away, the more excited I got. Going there for a year would make me so different to anyone I had ever known, and that had always been my goal.

The moment I arrived in Istanbul at my billeted home and a maid with carefully sculpted eyebrows and her hair swept neatly back into a chignon opened the door, my life changed completely. I felt like Annie when she first arrives at Daddy Warbucks's mansion. By some incredible fluke, my Turkish host family was extraordinarily wealthy and my new home was an eighteenth-century Ottoman palace, with more than sixty rooms, situated on the banks of the Bosphorus Strait. My host mum was in her late twenties and glamorous, with shiny black hair and sparkling eyes, and my host dad had an enormous handlebar moustache and a Harley. They had been educated in the United States and had decided to have an exchange student come and live with them to help their two children, who were aged six and four, learn English.

I wanted to be good, to please my new family and be loved by them, so I did all the right things. I was tidy and punctual and always offered to help. Every morning I waited outside to be picked up by the school bus and came straight home afterwards. I spoke English to the kids and accompanied them to birthday parties on the weekends. I wasn't quite a daughter and I wasn't quite the hired help: I was something in between.

But school got boring quickly. I had to go every day and yet the teachers didn't let me join in on any of the Turkish classes, only English and German. In my free periods I was sent to the art room to draw circles over and over on a sheet of white paper stuck to an easel or to sit in the tiny one-roomed library trying to read the Turkish newspaper. The school was a tall, bright blue building with an electronic gate that was operated by a security guard sitting in a little booth. At the start and end of the school day he pressed a button that made it slide open, and if you wanted to leave outside of those hours you had to get a permission slip. As an exchange student it wasn't too hard to talk my way out though, making excuses of outside lessons or commitments in broken Turkish.

And then I started wagging school completely, so instead of catching the private school bus brimming with the wealthy offspring of famous fashion designers and politicians and their mechanical practice English conversations, I caught the dolmuş by myself with normal people headed the opposite direction into the city each day. The minibus meandered alongside the strait and up through the clattering streets of Beşiktaş to Taksim Square, where I tumbled out and breathed in the chestnuts roasting, the corn on the cob and my favourite, the toasted simit—a Turkish bagel. I spent my day walking around the city and always ended it in one of the poky old cinemas, watching Hollywood movies with Turkish subtitles.

I became aware of how different the teenagers were there, how much more worldly they seemed because of living in a big city. They appeared to be obsessed with fashion in a way I had never been. In Buderim everyone wore surf brands or hippie clothes—long skirts and tight singlets, hoop earrings, leather sandals. Turkish people, rich or poor, coveted expensive American luxury brands, and they commented on my blue eyes constantly, telling me how beautiful they were. It was such a different idea to beauty from mine. I had never noticed eye colour before; to me, eyes were all the same.

My Turkish school friends had at first been puzzled by my Australianness, and one day at lunchtime when we were sitting on a hallway radiator, trying to stay warm and eating cheese toasties, they tried to pin down which nationality I resembled most.

'She's like an American,' said Deniz, chewing gum and twisting her drink straw round and round until it snapped.

'No, she's more European,' insisted Büçke.

'No, she's not like either of them,' said Zeynep, studying me carefully. 'Australians are something else completely different.' I wished she could explain to me exactly what that was but the bell shrilled and we had to hurry back to class.

In Istanbul, you're always in between something. I was enthralled by the idea that one moment I could be in Europe and twenty minutes later I could be in Asia. A foot on each continent. When I was out there on the ferry it was easy to imagine I was nowhere and everywhere. I tried to convince myself of the significance of being in between two continents, of being so close to both but not actually grounded on either one. It seemed too much to grasp; my mind would tire of the effort and I always got distracted by what was in front of me: the blue-green of the water, the pungent smell of fish, the elegance of the historic wooden palaces that lined the strait, the yalıs. The sound of traffic as I got closer to the shore of the eastern side and then the scramble to disembark, how sometimes my bum would be pinched by a slimy guy in the crowded rush to get off and for the rest of the day I'd be in a bad mood, afraid, upset and just angry, distrustful of everyone.

I was seventeen and dreamt of love, but the relationships between men and women being played out on the streets outside the palace walls seemed terrifying. Where women walked, men stared. Often when I passed a group of guys, they muttered something under their breath I didn't understand. Was it the equivalent of a wolf whistle or a tsk tsk? Did it mean I impressed them or shamed them? Sometimes the men's attention felt like appreciation and sometimes it felt like disgust. I couldn't read it. I could never find anything disrespectful about the way I presented myself; when I went outside I overdid it on purpose, covering up completely with oversized coats and sunglasses. I even dyed my hair a wishy-washy brown and hurried through the squares filled with men, head down, ignoring anyone who approached.

A few times I was followed, trailed, by a solitary man. Once it was a guy in a car, as I walked all the way down the hill from my school to home. At first I stayed calm and patient, and continued walking, ignoring him. But at the bottom of the hill, still sensing his creeping presence a metre behind me I turned around and screamed indignantly, 'What are you doing?!' in Turkish. He gave me a smarmy smile and sped off, seeming satisfied that he'd upset me. It wasn't the only time, and it made me hyper-sensitive to any sort of attention—even if someone just looked at me I hated it. I was confused. All my life I'd wanted attention and now that I was getting lots of it I didn't like it.

Every single day I wrote letters to my other family, the one left behind in Buderim. The week I had arrived was the same week Princess Diana died and I wrote as if the position had become available. 'I feel like a princess trapped in a palace, too,' I scrawled. I always referred to the place I lived in as 'The Palace'. I delighted in telling my Buderim family all about the swimming pool in the living room, the elevator that took you up three floors, the many spiral staircases with blue-glass balustrades, the salon full of priceless antiques and the romantic white gazebo in the rose garden, just like the one out of *The Sound of Music*, where I watched the boats on the Bosphorus go sailing past. It seemed like an incredible dream, something I would really appreciate one day, when I was older, when I wasn't spending all my energy each day just trying to find out where I fit.

At breakfast each morning I ate bread hot from the oven with many different sorts of cheeses, and olives, tomato and honey. In the evenings, dinner was served early for the kids and the adults ate later. I wasn't a kid or an adult, so I ate meals at both. In fact, I ate all the time. A new feeling— loneliness—made me ravenous. In ten weeks I gained ten kilograms. My parents' fears of me starving while away on exchange seemed ridiculous now.

One day the cook and the babysitter who worked at The Palace asked me to go out with them on their day off. They led me through the back streets of the wealthy suburb we lived in, past the local mosque with its manicured garden and behind the middle-class apartment blocks, through twisting unpaved streets where washing hung from the balconies of crooked-leaning apartments and the dust from the street scuffed up underneath our feet. We sat down on three wooden boxes that were positioned slightly off the road, a ratty tarpaulin hanging above us as a sun shelter. We were brought tea and sweets by a woman wearing a headscarf and plastic shoes. Music played from a tinny radio, and as skinny children ran around us my friends started chatting much more loudly and more confidently than I'd ever seen them behave at home, where they were always reserved and submissive. I tried to listen and follow their conversation but then they were suddenly standing and singing and dancing in a boisterous ring around the table. They made me get up and demonstrated how I should move my hips to the music, then grabbed my hands and pulled me around with them in a dizzying circle. My Turkish family often took me to brunches at ritzy hotels, to private swimming clubs and to upmarket, catered children's birthday parties with jumping castles and roving entertainment, but this was the most fun I'd had since I'd arrived.

But by the end of the year I felt like I'd transformed from a butterfly into a caterpillar. The clothes I wore, the way I walked down the street, had changed. Sometimes I tried to go out and exercise, but every time I went for a jog I'd get stared at by curious onlookers who weren't used to seeing people exercising in public. By the time I left I felt really grown up: I'd learnt that life could be lonely and yet exciting, immensely rich and yet indescribably poor. I said goodbye to my Istanbul family, feeling unsure about who I was now. I didn't know what I wanted anymore.

When I got back to Buderim I was eighteen and my face and body felt bulkier, puffier, older. Kat came back and she'd changed as well. She seemed to have a real focus, a direction. For the first time in my life, I went quiet. I didn't clamber for attention. I no longer fit into my old clothes so I had to start experimenting. I went through Mum's cupboards which were like enormous dress-up boxes. She always kept everything. Dresses she'd only half-finished making with pins still stuck in them like voodoo dolls, her old clothes from when she was a teenager, as well as maternity smocks in fabulous sixties prints and sparkly costumes she'd made for our community theatre shows. I took away anything shiny or floral or colourful. Long gypsy skirts. Bright floral blouses. And dresses. So many dresses.

Xanthe and Analiese had left home and taken their double act to Brisbane to both study drama at university. They lived in a sharehouse together and wore glamorous scarves and jackets and hats like people did in Europe. When they came home on weekends to visit us, they brought with them the play scripts and textbooks they were working on at uni and I flicked through them, annoyed that I was still living at home. Everything here seemed the same, but I was different. The old frustration of missing out, of my sisters always getting to where I wanted to be before me, was back. The house felt so empty now with just me and Lachy in it. I couldn't wait to leave again.

Mum's old clothes quickly became my uniform. Whenever I got bored with what I was wearing, I plucked more clothes from her never-ending supply. These were Hydra wardrobes: more dresses would grow from where I took the last. There was a sense of mystery to Mum's wardrobe. When I asked her where this or that piece came from, she sighed and said: 'Oh, I don't know, Lorelei! They just *appeared*.'

But the real reason was that as Xanthe and Analiese got tired of what they were wearing, they came back home and filled the holes that had been left when they moved out with all the clothes they didn't want anymore. In this way, I saw many of the clothes that would make up my wardrobe modelled by other women first, either my sisters or my mum. Seeing clothes on them, I could reconfigure them in my mind, mould them onto my shape, a different shape—less bust here, shorter waist—but in the same way you see a movie star on the screen and put yourself in their body, your face becoming their face, I could imagine myself into these clothes by seeing them on Xanthe and Analiese first.

Xanthe had the figure of a shop mannequin. I admired her and coveted everything she wore. And it was Xanthe, who was truly magazine fashionable and who shed clothes every single season, who I waited behind quietly to catch the debris. She discarded everything—upgraded, up-seasoned—and I grabbed anything I could carry, took her old dresses in my arms and held onto them tight, wanting to keep it all, keep our family together when she, the first, left home and nothing seemed the same anymore. Using safety pins, sashes and ribbons, I made her clothes fit me.

On the morning I finally moved to my own place, I was reunited with a dress I had forgotten about in the back of Mum's wardrobe. One of the yellow butterfly-catchers' dresses that had been made for an eleven-year-old girl. I tried it on. Standing in my mum's wardrobe, in the too-tight dress made for my sisters, the memory of singing with Kat came back. I remembered the world before Istanbul, the person I had been. In just a year I had changed so much, but wearing the dress I felt like I was myself again. I wanted *something*.

It was the first year of my twenties, and a friend who was helping me move my stuff to Brisbane arrived to pick me up. Mum and Dad were stressed, trying to help me pack, and I felt annoyed at them, irritated that it had taken so long for my life to start. I got changed, cramming the yellow dress into my already over-stuffed duffel bag. We loaded up the ute with my bed, my books and my dresses, and I kissed my parents and said goodbye. I remembered the last time we'd parted, at the airport eighteen months earlier, how I wasn't really sure if I was ready to fly away yet and be on my own, and their gentle confidence that I'd be fine. This time was different: I was just impatient to leave and start my life.

'Be good,' said Dad.

'Be sane,' said Mum.

Twenty

I had a party at my new house to celebrate my birthday. Friends from uni came and we all packed into the small living room and kitchen, tumbling out onto the verandah and making so much noise the neighbours complained. People wandered in and out of my bedroom that was strewn with all the clothes I could never fit into the built-in wardrobes, so instead I left them hanging on the backs of chairs and thrown on the floor. My books overflowed on the shelves. I loved having everything out on show, because that way people could immediately know who I was.

It was my first sharehouse: my housemates, Ady and Noe and Carly, and I shared everything. Cooking and clothes and cab rides home. Gossip and books and one portable CD player we moved between each other's rooms. We hung up white bedsheets in the living room and did a photo shoot wearing each other's dresses. We sat on each other's beds in the mornings with tea and toast and talked until lunchtime about our nights out before. Snuggled cosily among these girls my age, with normal things like boys and uni to talk about, I could shed the protective layers I'd covered myself with in Turkey and at last feel grown-up and like myself.

I carried a book around with me everywhere as a compass to lead me towards new friends. Whenever I met someone, I pulled it out of my handbag and asked if they had read it. If they had I instantly loved them. It was *Franny and Zooey* by J.D. Salinger. I'd first discovered it in the public library when I was fourteen and had felt so attached to it I never returned it. I loved the character of Franny, a student actor fixated on the world of artifice. The book still rang as true to me as it did when I had first discovered it, but now it had also become a beacon that guided me in the direction of what I wanted to be too: an actor.

But I was determined to find a way to get there without copying my sisters. All through school I had been known as Xanthe and Analiese's little sister, and I didn't want that to happen at uni. I wanted to be known in my own right. So I had a clever idea. I thought if I could write films I could star in them, like Woody Allen, and that would be my way in. So I had enrolled in a creative writing degree. It was a roundabout way to get there, but at least I wouldn't be an identical cut-out paper-doll sister. Mum and Dad were relieved by this decision—they thought that it might even lead to me becoming a journalist, which was an actual real job. My two sisters struggled for acting work. They had part-time employment working at a children's fairy shop where they dressed up in wings and glitter and told stories. This sounded like fun to me, but interviewing people and writing about them was so much more of a *real* career.

One of my electives was Film and TV Scriptwriting. I knew I wanted to write stories about a young girl's search for her identity in a world gone mad, films featuring smart, creative young women, films like *Annie Hall*. But that semester we were stuck studying real life: documentary.

Our assignment was a fifteen-minute interview for a documentary, and to do that we had to find a subject worth documenting. All my friends talked a lot about doing things as they drank casks of red wine, but no one actually did anything worth chronicling for posterity. Then I remembered my high-school friend Beck. She and her boyfriend Mark were running a café and music venue called the Pot Music Bar. It wasn't a shabby makeshift place either: it was a proper venue, enclosed with floor-to-ceiling windows, and situated at the bottom of a block of corporate offices in Paddington, away from the live music precincts of Fortitude Valley and West End. There was no one else my age who was doing anything as cool as that, and when I called her up she said yes.

I borrowed a brick-sized dictaphone from the university journalism department and put a cassette in it. I got on a bus I had never caught before and stepped out onto Petrie Terrace, a winding, fairytale-like thoroughfare situated at the top of a hill. I felt nervous. I had to remind myself: this is just Beck. But she was running a *café*. A place people went to, that bands played at. Plus she had an older boyfriend. She had quit university. She was meeting famous local musicians.

Beck had cut her hair in a Gertrude Stein style: dark, cap-like fronds gripping to her head, like the petals of an unbloomed tulip. Her dark eyes were set inside black-framed glasses. Her hair, those frames and the beauty mark on her cheek stood out like someone pressing too hard on a pencil. Her clothes were crinkled but the creases seemed to mould themselves to her body, like the toga of a classical statue, crafted and artfully deliberate.

I took out my notebook. This did feel like a proper job, like I *was* a journalist. I felt a moment of pride: maybe this writing thing would actually work. Maybe I would someday be the daughter who had a proper career that earnt money!

Beck was always moving, always in the middle of an action. Lighting a cigarette. Greeting someone. Taking a phone call. Making a coffee. As she walked around, I followed her and scribbled down notes so I could pepper my documentary script with interesting and artistic observations.

It was a heady time in Brisbane, though I didn't become aware of it until I started hanging out at the Pot. I asked if I could help and started working there for free, a pad and pen stuck in my apron pocket, and took orders and bussed food out to customers. Waitressing seemed the same thing as acting. Wearing a cute costume, tricking people into thinking you were someone you weren't, being hyper-friendly and smiling so much that by the end of the day your jaw ached.

During the day the music was Elvis, James Taylor and the *Forrest Gump* soundtrack, to suit the corporate customers who spent their lunch breaks eating paninis and having business meetings. But right on 6 p.m. Beck put on some French electronica or experimental stuff until that night's band had set up.

During my interview with Beck she told me that Brisbane's live music scene was endangered by some swanky new apartment blocks that had been built in Fortitude Valley, the music hub on the fringe of the city. Individual residents and opportunistic competing businesses were trying to shut down music venues through the liquor licensing commission, and the situation was intensifying as protests began. Noise complaints started to kill off all the original live music venues. The Pot was joining the fight.

'It's really hard. There've been five different cafés in this space over one and a half years, and none of them have been able to stay open for very long,' Beck told me.

'Well, how are *you guys* going to survive?' I asked, genuinely puzzled by how she expected to make it work.

'Well, as Mark says, it all comes down to budgeting, to cutting things out that aren't important,' she sighed. 'Prioritising the important things.' It seemed very grown up. I scribbled it down and underlined it emphatically as though it was the secret to life.

As well as running the Pot, Beck performed in a band with Pete, who was only a few years older than us. He had been our high-school music teacher for a short time. He'd introduced African gospel songs to brighten up our regular dull choral repertoire, songs with beats and vibrant harmonies; he played us Björk in music class, and was destined for some life beyond being just a music teacher. The band was called Smear: S & M for the ear, and they played 'industrial ambience'. I had just discovered Patti Smith's *Horses* and was inspired to start writing poetry, rhymes and word play that I'd tie together in one long poem. I practised reading the poems out loud in my bedroom when my housemates weren't there. I liked fitting the words together so they tripped off each other and ran together like an unstoppable river.

Before the night of my first performance at the Institute of Modern Art, I went round to the Pot early so Beck could give me a pep talk. I was really nervous. It felt like this was it. The moment I had been building towards, when the words

I had written would put me back on the stage where I could perform. I practised the poem in front of her, enunciating the final line with great theatrical gravity:

'And although I no longer skip, my CDs still do. Blood's on my lip, left over from you.'

There was a long pause. 'Oh my god,' she said. 'Lorelei, that is amazing.'

'Really? You think so?'

She nodded vigorously, always supportive and encouraging of everything I did.

I burst into tears.

'What's wrong? The poem is really good!'

I exclaimed, 'I know! It's totally scary how good that is! What if I can't handle being that good? It's so much pressure.' As I dissolved into sobs and allowed the full gravitas of being so brilliant at something overwhelm me, Beck wordlessly hugged me. She got it.

I started playing shows on weekends with Smear, incorporating my beat poetry with Pete's music and Beck's vocals. We rehearsed in Pete's bedroom every week and made films to be projected behind us when we performed, and created costumes to wear each night. Sometimes our friend Hannah made dresses for us from fabric we found at op shops; other times we just threw together what we had, our combined dress styles coming together on stage in a cacophony of patterns and colours and shapes. For our gig at the 4ZZZ market day, at a park in West End, I wore a tennis skirt as a top safety-pinned around my bust, and a pair of men's tiny footy shorts with red high heels. I moved to the front to do my poetry, and afterwards Beck took centre stage while I danced behind her, my platinum blonde pigtails whipping back and forth as I tried to stop my tennis-skirt top from falling down, equal parts thrilled and astonished that people in the audience were on their feet and dancing too. They really liked this stuff.

Performing in Smear was different to when I was a kid doing a play and we had to learn lines from a script. This was our own work: we had written it ourselves and we were performing it. I felt like I was achieving my Woody Allen ideal where I could be writer, director and performer all at once. How majestic it felt to be completely in control. I knew the band wasn't just about me—I didn't write the music or sing—but I still felt like a ruler over my little realm of poetry.

As the venues started closing down, everything became do-it-yourself. We practised and performed in our own homes and backyards because there was nowhere else to do it. If Sydney and Melbourne were the two older sisters who got all the attention, Brisbane was the third one who got away with doing heaps of crazy stuff because no one was watching. Beck and I decided to put on a show at her house one night and bought paintbrushes and paper and typewriters and casks of wine, and opened up the house to the general public to come and watch us perform and paint and type. I'd once thought Iceland was the most artistic and bohemian enclave in the world, but here in Brisbane I'd found the energy and creative life I'd always fantasised about.

Each week after we finished rehearsing, I walked home through the streets of Highgate Hill looking into the lit-up houses like it was a show on TV; for the first time, it felt like I wasn't watching life anymore. I was in it, centre stage, making my own things and putting them out into the world.

I didn't have much money, but I spent whatever I did have on music. The Golden Palominos, Björk, P.J. Harvey, Fiona Apple, Patti Smith. It was becoming clear that money was finite and if you spent it on one thing, you couldn't spend it on another. My parents had decided to pay all four of their children's rent for the duration of their degrees, with the expectation that we would all get part-time jobs as well. But I was too busy working for free.

So I came up with a brilliant solution. I had learnt from Beck and Mark that when money and art clashed, you had to cut something out, you had to budget. I wondered what I could cut out of my life to save money. The answer came back loud and clear: dairy.

Veganism felt like my fate. I'd been thinking about it for a while, but it suddenly became the solution to my money problems as well. The only person I'd heard of who was vegan was Daniel Johns from the band Silverchair. I didn't know anyone vegan in real life, so just like everything else at the time, I made it up myself.

Veganism, to me, was all about cutting things out. No more cheese, which was an extravagant luxury. But instead of replacing it with tofu, or milk with soy milk, or eggs with nuts, which would have been way too expensive, I simply stopped eating almost everything, and lived off dry biscuits, pasta sprinkled with salt, and apples.

Some people 'become' vegan, as if it's a natural stage of life they enter. Some people 'go' vegan, as if it's an airline. But I 'turned' vegan, like into a werewolf: I shifted into my new form overnight and with a maniacal glint in my eyes. Turning vegan made me feel like I was a person of substance, like I stood for things and knew who I was.

I was losing weight, but it didn't bother me. Artists were supposed to be thin. The musicians and artists I idolised lived on alcohol and cigarettes anyway. I was still self-conscious of the weight I'd put on two years earlier in Turkey, and was secretly pleased that my dresses now needed taking in.

I spent every night I could at the Pot, manning the door,

drinking gin from a water bottle at my feet, watching the bands and scribbling down lines of poetry in my notebook.

Tonight I will sit in this place for a few hours pouring sugar into my cup, my Ceylon bop, each drop awakening my foreign genealogy. These faces of men, white and shaved this morning. Already splades of black have appeared like a dark halo around their chin. Illuminated by the cherry of their cigarettes as they drag, and they drag their dates into the boardroom: the convention room. In their suits, they suit each other, resolute and united in a delighted love of this— working on a Friday night. Time passes quickly on my neighbourhood watch.

At university, I'd heard about the ultimate artistic gathering: the National Young Writers' Festival in Newcastle. For one week this surfing town on the New South Wales coast brimmed with writers and musicians and artists. I had to go.

Newcastle was a ten-hour drive away and I caught a lift with a friend named Liberty, who was a year or two older than me and studying film and photography. By the time we got there, the town had filled up with people from all over the country and there was no accommodation left, so we pitched a tent in someone's backyard. For three days and nights, I wore my most bohemian dresses—a long blue wrap skirt covered with large red and yellow flowers, Mum's paisley pink shift dress, a neon yellow smock that barely covered my bum. I attended panels and writers' discussions and was too busy meeting people to bother searching out nutritional vegan food, so I filled up on ginger beer and chips. I stayed out late and talked to everyone, dragging myself home to the tent at the end of the night only when there was no one else left.

I prepared some of my poetry to read out at the open mic events, where there were only ever a few people listening cross-legged on the floor. I spent the weekend gobsmacked that normal people like me could get so close to famous authors like Christos Tsiolkas and Linda Jaivin. I had never seen myself fitting in at a writers' festival; my sisters had set no precedent for this.

On the last day of the festival, I started to feel really sick. I thought I was just hungover and hungry. We packed everything back up into the car and as soon as I finally located a savoury vegan muffin and devoured it I knew that I wouldn't be able to keep it down. I held out until just outside of Newcastle before I started vomiting. I could feel the muscles of my stomach tighten and then loosen. I yelled out to stop the car. Every hour until we got to Brisbane I had to get out to vomit. It was the longest drive I had ever been on.

I was dropped home and fell straight into bed in the dress I was wearing, a light cotton print with a long, billowing skirt. I'd been wearing it for two days, and it now smelt dirty with fever-sweat and spew. I lay there in panic and pain, all night, having never felt so wretched, still vomiting bile into a saucepan regularly. First thing the next day, with no recovery in sight, my housemates still asleep and no idea of what else to do, I called my parents. They showed up on my doorstep exactly an hour later, and bundled me into the car.

I watched as the city sped past. In the shuttering light, the world passed by through the windows like the frames of a film. Brisbane looked so small and colonial, like it was just starting up. The comforting sirens of the city got softer and we sped out of the city, back towards home. I sprawled in the back seat like a child, feeling light as a hot air balloon. I went in and out of consciousness. At one point I wound down the window. One of the straps of my dress fell off my shoulder. The dress was one of Mum's early pieces, made before she knew how to put a zipper in, so instead she attached purple pea-like buttons that ran up the back. It seemed weird to think that Mum used to be so young she didn't know how to put a zipper in. In the front, she and Dad were talking quietly to each other. We took an unfamiliar turn-off from the highway and I realised we were driving straight to the emergency ward of Nambour Hospital. I hadn't even noticed things had turned so out of control.

My balloon skirt breathed in and out as we sped along, flapping and fluttering. The images of women holding up parasols, the men twiddling canes, moved with the breeze. I loved those pictures: there was a sense that they were on the edge of something, full of promise and expectation, about to soar up somewhere completely undiscovered.

In the foyer of the hospital the doctor prodded my arm with his thumbs, pressing hard in to the skin and yelling, 'We can't find a vein!' like a TV doctor. And then I was in a wheelchair and someone lifted my dress off me and put me in a hospital smock and into a bed, and stuck a drip full of saline into my arm. I was told I was seriously malnourished and that I had to stay in hospital for three days. All year I'd revelled in making do with what was available, in living life as a do-it-yourself art project. Organising events, writing scripts and poetry, and putting on shows all by ourselves. But in the meantime I'd neglected the artistry it took to master the most basic pursuit: survival. What a delicate art, I thought as the saline pumped into me, just working out how much food you need to stay alive.

Twenty-one

We fell in love the night he came to see my band play. I saw him tall as an afternoon shadow by the bar and the next day he walked to my house and asked me on a date. We drove out to the suburbs, and I waited in the car at the service station as he filled up, thrilled just waiting to be taken somewhere.

He came back with pre-packaged ice-creams on sticks and we sat on a median strip underneath some power lines and guzzled them. I nuzzled into his chest and breathed in the smoky suede of his dad's too-large jacket and felt warm in the cool night air.

He drove me home and parked at the school opposite my sharehouse and turned up the volume on the Nirvana cassette. We swayed in the carpark and when he dipped me I squealed, like a babe in arms catching its first splash of waves.

Jack was studying to be an engineer but what he really wanted to do was play music. He rehearsed with his friends in the living room of an old Queenslander on top of the hill, a sharehouse hive of rooms where Beck lived too.

He had a boyish awkwardness: gangly and stretched out like a greyhound. A toothy grin and gigantic paws that took hold of my shoulders and melted them in one shake. He wore beautifully made old suits from op shops, paired them with secondhand cotton business shirts that had foreign labels. His clothes rarely fit his lanky body—his sleeves sometimes too short, sometimes too long—but he made his own alterations. Rolled-up sleeves, jackets undone. Always a thin striped arrow tied in a knot around his neck pointing down at his sneakers.

After we'd been dating for a few weeks, I went with him to the wedding of an old family friend of his. It was the first time I'd ever caught a bouquet, and afterwards we snuck away from the reception down to the beach. Norfolk pines stood like soldiers guarding the water and we sat close to each other on a picnic table. The sun went down as the squawks of lorikeets went up, and we watched the waves, like curtains rippling in the moonlight, sewing themselves a lacy trim. Above us the moon shone on.

When the holidays came, we drove out to far western Queensland to visit his parents. The further out we drove, the more the roadkill piled up. Surrounded by all that meat, I was worried about what I would eat out there, but when we arrived after ten hours on the road, sweaty and sore, his mum hugged me warmly and brought out a freshly baked zucchini slice.

His dad was an apiarist, and kept his bees out there in roo-shooting country where everything was bone-dry. He drove us around town as four-wheel drives prowled past us armoured with spotlights square like TVs but brighter, hunting kangaroos as pests. It made me feel sick. Ghost gums shimmied in the shy breeze, the land spat out yellow and red dirt like a roadworker's sign twirling never-endingly between SLOW and STOP. The creek, the smell of the bed, the sunbaked dirt scuffing against our calves, and always the lumbering, creaking awareness of something bigger than us out there, an ever-present crowing or laughing that came from above.

He was the first guy I brought home to meet my family and I wanted them to like him; I kept telling everyone he was studying to be an engineer to impress them, even though Jack didn't actually want to be an engineer and I loved him for being a musician. We dragged two single mattresses into my parents' living room to sleep but he was too shy to take his trousers off in case someone walked in, so he slept in them. When Dad discovered Jack was the son of a beekeeper, he asked for his help to extract the hives we kept on our property to pollinate the strawberries. Despite Jack's warnings about how to do it, Dad did it his own way and got stung all over his face and the skin around his eyes blew up puffy and red. Jack didn't get stung at all.

I took Jack to the beach where I had done junior lifesaving every weekend as a kid. I always hated it. The swimming cramps, ankles twisting on trapdoor sand, the shrill whistles, the hollering coaches. Teenagers wearing the maroon swimsuit of the surf club paddled by, in training, and Jack and I swam out beyond them, swirling in the deep together, my legs wrapped around him as he held both of us there. The shiny face of the sea, its thousands of sunlit eyelids closing and opening, paparazzi flashes, watching and not watching us kiss.

I was in my final year of uni, studying writing, film and French, and I shared all my classes with a guy named Paul, a mature-aged student in his late thirties with boyish blond curls and a warm, chipmunkish smile. When I met him in my first year of uni I was stand-offish with him, wary because I'd never had any adult, grown-up friends before, especially not grown men. But it quickly became clear that Paul was friends with everyone. He was known around campus for his khaki shorts, zany button-up shirts and high distinctions. One day, Paul ran into class excited. He'd just found out he had got an audition as a contestant on the gameshow *Sale of the Century*. He invited our whole writing class over to his house to play the board-game version so he could practise, and he showed off the five collared shirt-and-tie packs he'd bought from Lowes. 'They film the entire week's shows on the same day so if you get through to the next round you need to be prepared!' he told us.

Paul was always interested in what was going on in my life, where I came from and where I wanted to go. Talking to him made me feel like a grown-up, with legitimate goals. He also made me feel I had a story to tell. 'Tell me about Turkey,' he said comradely as we walked home along the quiet, coffee-coloured Brisbane River. So I told him of Istanbul's beauty, of the city and the sky, the noisy traffic, about the stray cats and the water that purred down the famous sleek waterway that separated Asia and Europe. I described the seagulls and fishermen. The kids swimming off the banks. The sugar cubes crumbling and dissolving into your tea, and the empty tulip glasses gathered on silver trays.

I wanted Paul to think me observant, a writer, an artist, someone who noticed things. I explained how I used to close my eyes to try to appreciate the significance of sailing on those famous waters, but it never lasted long. I always opened them again because life was on either side of me, on the land, on either bank. Here, on the water, wasn't a real place, it was just where you waited while you were being taken somewhere else.

Growing up, I was used to having the most hyperactive energy in the room, but working on group projects with Paul I found that for once I was the calm one. His enthusiasm for everything was almost over-the-top and he liked puns and word play as much as I did. And he always had lots of ideas.

When our uni group had to make a short film for assessment, he pitched his idea to us. 'This guy, a hitcher, is walking along with his thumb out and a kombivan full of hippies speeds past without stopping. Later on, he finds where the kombi is parked and gets his revenge by tinkering with the engine. Then he gets out from under the bonnet and continues on his way.' Paul was getting more animated and grinning excitedly in anticipation of the punchline. 'Cut to the kombi careening recklessly down a hill, and the frightened hippie driver discovers the brake isn't working. At the very last second we see the hitchhiker's shocked face that exact moment before the kombi collides into him, then the title of the film comes up—*Hit-cha!*'

Paul chuckled with glee. There was no competition—his idea was the best. We drove to Buderim to scout for film locations, and dropped in on my parents. Over cups of tea, Paul talked me up to my parents and made me proud that I was kicking goals at uni. I was a little embarrassed, but also pleased by all the stuff he remembered, and how he presented me as an intelligent, thoughtful, creative person to my family.

I got a high distinction for my role in our short film, and every other assignment I collaborated with Paul on.

Jack and I lived in separate sharehouses where the telephones were constantly being shut off, so we wrote letters to each other and left them in a secret letterbox opposite the Night Owl, a convenience store at the juncture of the two streets that led in opposite directions to our houses. We'd leave love notes folded and hidden in a small hollow below a billboard advertising Killer Pythons, letters scribbled on the backs of electricity bills and shopping dockets. At the end of even the shortest letter Jack always wrote that he loved me. I'd jump off the bus and rush over to collect my secret mail and, reading those words, I felt excited for all the things we hadn't had a chance to do together yet.

We were crazy, dippy, mad about each other. We called each other baby, darling schmarling, honey, and he always told me I was a library of beauty. 'How do you say that in French?' he asked me one day, and I looked it up in my dictionary word for word and wrote it back to him in a letter. *'Tu es une bibliothèque de beauté!'* Before I delivered it to the

Killer Python letterbox, I checked the sentence with Paul. He corrected the accents above the 'e's which I always got the wrong way round.

Jack and I nestled in close to each other wherever we went. Sometimes just to see what would happen, I'd go loose in his arms to surprise him. He would buckle trying to hold my weight. He was so tall that I strained my neck when I kissed him. I had to stand on tiptoe for my mouth to get to his, and it was a cute problem to have. Being in love with him felt like a show we put on for an adoring public.

Not much had happened in our lives, but we spent the hours we were together trying to find out everything that had. Ever since Paul encouraged me, I was caught up in this tale of Turkey and wanted to talk about it. It was the biggest thing that had ever happened to me, the thing that made me stand out. Now I found myself weaving a different tale for Jack compared to the one I told Paul, trying to demonstrate to both of them who I was; discovering that stories have different purposes depending on who you're telling them to.

'Tell me about your life,' Jack would say as we lay in bed on a rainy winter morning, and I told him how in Istanbul I felt so confused and stuck between worlds. I described the Aya Sofya, which started out as a church and then became a mosque and was now a museum, which proved that anything could become something else if you waited long enough.

I wanted Jack to find me bewitching and brave, so I told him the other stories, the ones about men. I told Jack about how they stared and the strategies I had developed, trying to turn myself from the watched into the watcher. But no matter how determined I was, I always ended up looking away first.

I told Jack that when I was in Istanbul I just wanted to be in love with a person like I was in love with Istanbul, passionately and dramatically. The city didn't love you back like a man might. He asked me if I had been in love, before now, before him. I said I wasn't sure—maybe—and told him about Esteban.

Esteban was one of my fellow exchange students, a Paraguayan who lived down on the west coast. When we had met at a mid-year exchange-student camp, my life in Turkey finally started to come together. He spoke no English and I spoke no Spanish but we both spoke a bit of Turkish. He told me that one of my eyes was beautiful (he hadn't grasped plurals yet) and I murmured seductively that there was a cow on board the bus (I meant to say this is our stop). But our lips understood each other and when he visited Istanbul to see me near the end of my trip, our Turkish had improved and we both spoke with more confidence. Which is how I discovered I didn't actually want to talk to him, I just wanted to kiss.

Kissing is really hard to do in Istanbul. There was always someone watching. I would never have attempted it near a mosque or in a smaller neighbourhood, but right in the centre of the city, in the square at the top of İstiklal Caddesi, Independence Avenue, it seemed okay. I'd seen other teenagers in school uniforms hanging out there; some of them even held hands.

I took Esteban there and, hidden on a small bench behind a bush, I threw my arms around his neck and I started kissing him. He pulled away. In broken Turkish, struggling like we all did to get the word order correct, he said, 'Stop we should, or police will come.'

I looked around. I knew we wouldn't actually get arrested for pashing in Taksim Square but I was feeling nervous too. Anxiety was a normal state since I'd arrived. Everyone's parents made them watch *Midnight Express* before they went to Turkey and if I looked further down the street I could see the rows of police wearing masks and shields, who were always stationed in this area of the city to watch over protests.

But they couldn't see us right now, so I snuggled into him closer on the park bench and swung my legs over his. He pushed me away again and told me he didn't want to get arrested. I realised he was genuinely worried. But I didn't care anymore. I was trying to be good and follow all the rules, but people still stared no matter what. The rules seemed contradictory. I hated feeling like strangers controlled what I could and couldn't do. I was sick of being scared. In a spontaneous, reckless hormone-fuelled moment, I climbed onto his lap, trying to find out what he was made of, but he pushed me away with a fierceness that jolted me back in shock.

I stepped away and headed off down the street, not sure whether to leave or to return. I was ashamed, rejected, stung. I hurled myself into the hordes of other people on İstiklal Caddesi. I wanted to get lost in them. I pushed myself past people, blinking away the tears. My Latin lover wasn't living up to his stereotype; what, I wondered, was mine? That western women are easy? That's the understanding I'd eventually absorbed in every man's stare.

I felt a tugging on my elbow and swung around furiously, anticipating the usual harassment and preparing an angry response in Turkish. It was Esteban. He pulled me in close and pressed his lips to my cheek. 'To stay in a room tonight. Will you help me find?' he asked. I smiled as I felt the warmth of his mouth on mine. 'Yes,' I whispered beguilingly. 'There is a hotels available in these back streets I have heard.'

He took my hand and we went searching. We found one we liked the look of, but when we asked to see the room the landlord looked me up and down. 'No girls allowed,' he barked.

'But his sister I am!' I insisted. 'And check the room I must, to make sure they are suitable.'

As soon as we closed the door we started kissing again and peeling off each other's clothes. We were half undressed when we heard the stomping of several pairs of footsteps and then yelling and banging on the locked door.

Maybe you could really get arrested for being in a man's room and trying to have sex with him, I pondered. Especially if you're his sister. I checked the window in case there was a drainpipe to shimmy down but we were four flights up.

As we tried to get our clothes back on, the door sprang open and a crowd of men leered in on us. They must have been guys who worked there at the hotel, all in their twenties and thirties, five or more of them crammed together on the narrow landing of the staircase outside our room, all craning their necks to look in as the landlord shouted at us in Turkish.

I was scared; I was angry. But that was normal. I'd become accustomed in Turkey to feeling so many contradictory feelings at the same time.

I grabbed my bag and Esteban's hand and barged past the pack of bullies, and after spending almost a year of feeling like I had no control over how people treated me in public, I unleashed on them a stark, raving, LOTE hissy fit.

'What did you think we were doing, making the sex? Crazy you are, aren't you? I was doing the jump on the bed and seeing if the comfort was high. Come, my brother, we will never shop here again!'

The crowd parted as Esteban and I sailed out of there on the sheer hysterical force of my voice. He and I were so terrified we split up quickly, kissing each other goodbye in the middle of the crowded street and not caring who stared.

The next day the exchange organisation found out that Esteban had come to Istanbul without permission and he was sent back to Izmir. A few weeks later I got a letter from him, and at the end he wrote that he loved me. Reading those words I felt sad for all the things we hadn't had a chance to do together.

I watched him disappear into the crowd and started making my way down to the water, dreading the long ferry ride ahead, squashed in with the peak-hour crowds as we rumbled up the Bosphorus. Passing by an alleyway I saw a dress hanging up in a crammed shop, an Ali Baba's cave, surrounded by other treasures. It looked like a dress to conquer in. It had Aztec eyes. Vintage seventies, from Italy, the chic salesgirl told me. It felt soft and feathery but looked glacially metallic; its other-worldly tassels moved with me as I playfully wriggled around in it in front of the mirror while the salesgirl cooed, '*Çok güzel!* Very beautiful!' It was much too expensive but I put it on the credit card Dad had given me for emergencies.

At the time, it didn't seem to even fit me. I didn't know how to do up the top, a strange wrap design that seemed to be missing a clasp: tangle them up, dangle them, do whatever works. But in my mind there existed some grown-up version of myself that would wear it when I returned to Australia, an idea that came to me wrapped up in the tissue paper when I bought it. For me, this dress was hope, it was who I'd be when I got home, what I would become.

I was wearing it all those years later on stage, the night Jack and I fell in love, its dangling threads quivering like civilisations. Tassles tickling me like first love, and the wampum bam against my hips. The sea, the reeling and twirling and near-drowning as I swished through the crowd to where he stood at the bar. I wore it many more times that year; it finally fit, it finally made sense. I worked out how to wrap it and adapt it to my body. How to pull the skirt up so it sat a bit higher than it was designed to, to mask my short waist and make the dimensions more even. With Jack's arms around me, a willing audience, listening and laughing at my stories, I felt like I was home at last. I could tell him anything and he would love me.

Tu es une bibliothèque de beauté! That's still the sentence that rushes through my mind like water slicing through the strait, and I remember my old uni friend Paul, grinning, kindly correcting the accents over my 'e's, always encouraging me to tell more of my stories and noticing things about myself I hadn't seen. How he also showed me that men could be kind, that they could be friends, that they could be trusted.

After we all graduated I heard he became a presenter on ABC radio, an interviewer, and I knew he would be perfect at that. And I remember a while later, after I hadn't seen him for years and I was living in a different city, I was sitting in my car outside my house about to turn the key when I got a call from a friend telling me that he'd ended his own life, and I realised in astonishment then that I'd hardly known anything about him. For three years at uni he'd always listened to me talk, with his face lit up like a flashbulb, but I never thought to ask him much about himself. He was always the one who had the questions. Suddenly my night at the movies didn't seem so important. I got out of the car and went back inside, turned on all the lights, and made a cup of tea. As I watched the sugar dissolve I recalled those uni years. I'd felt so caught in those in-between waters separating two places, always waiting to get taken somewhere else, with no idea I was already there.

Twenty-two

On the day I graduated from uni I tore off the voluminous skirt and puffed sleeves of a pink satin eighties bridesmaid's dress. I wore the remaining frilled underskirt and bodice to the graduation ceremony, where I discovered the dress accidentally matched the fuchsia silk band of my graduate robe and cap. It was a good sign. Everything seemed pink and rosy, and afterwards I celebrated with my friends Romy and Rhianna, even though none of us had any idea what we would do now with a creative writing degree.

The next day, I painted my lips bright red and worked my first shift as a candy-bar girl at the local cinema. From that day on I lived in my sky-blue uniform. I smiled cheerfully and reminded every customer that, for just an extra fifty cents, they could upgrade their soft drink and popcorn to a mega-maxi combo. I tore tickets and walked down aisles to check the emergency exits, a quick push on the door to make sure people could escape.

If it was a quiet night, I scribbled fragments of stories on the backs of ticket stubs but usually tore them up too. I kept winning customer service awards at work: a voucher to spend at a department store, a weekend away on the Gold Coast. But the awards I wanted to win were for the writing competitions I submitted entries to on my days off, plays and poems and short stories. I never did.

Jack and I were living together in a building called Morroville. The name sounded to me like a city of tomorrow; I thought I could see our future in it. It looked like Old Hollywood—glamorous, with ivy climbing up its stone exterior, creaking windows that pushed straight out to let the day pour in, a rickety back staircase that led to our top-floor apartment, the little oblong of song where the vinyl vocals of my favourite singers (Slick, Flack, Nicks) scuffed the walls.

Both of us owned too many clothes and we filled our bedroom with things to hang them on. A standing hanger for Jack's jackets, another wiry one on wheels for his cardigans. A dresser with obstinate drawers was crammed full of underwear that poked out like tongues.

Of all the strange objects I'd fallen in love with and dragged home from an op shop, the Japanese dressing frame, wooden and heavy, was the most impractical. But when I had seen her I wanted her so badly. She comprised just three rectangular frames joined together in a concertina by rusty hinges, and now stood in the corner of the room alongside our tall mirror. I overloaded her with dresses so she leaned to one side like an old woman eavesdropping. The entire structure would topple if the dresses ever became unbalanced so I had to be careful to redistribute the weight after each depluming.

On weekends Jack and I hunted for secondhand records, crockery, board games, clothes. The classifieds section in the Saturday newspaper was our map, and Jack highlighted all the outer suburban garage sales before we left. My best finds were a big old black birdcage and a vintage red tea set with poppies painted all over it. In the birdcage we put a canary we called Gus, and in the teacups we poured Earl Grey tea. The teacups were tiny, but Jack still put three sugar cubes in each one like he was drinking from a mug.

We had bright mornings, the sun streaming in from the eastern sunroom, highlighting Gus's buttery plumage and spreading warmth through the whole house. A friend told me about a book that helped you rediscover your creativity called *The Artist's Way*. I made fun of it at first because it seemed so new age and corny, but as my days at the cinema got longer and I lost touch with my friends from uni, I started taking it more seriously. One of the daily exercises in the book was called the morning pages, which were three pages of stream-of-consciousness writing you were meant to do in the morning, but sometimes I spent all day on them because I wanted them to be really good. Jack would try to get me out of the house on my day off, to go have a beer or a walk in the park, but I refused. 'I have to do my morning pages,' I'd tell him.

'You know, you can't get graded on life,' Jack would say. 'You don't need to get perfect marks anymore. It doesn't work like that.'

But still I studied and worked like I'd always done, hoping if I did I might graduate to the next level.

I always had trouble getting ready when we went out at night. The late hours of the afternoon were spent doing and redoing my hair, changing shoes and stockings. I'd try something on and it wouldn't feel right so I'd have to change it. When it still wasn't right I'd go back to what I had before.

It was a feeling rather than a look that I was after; I couldn't explain what I was trying to achieve but when I hit on it I knew. It was, in a word, perfection. Whenever I appeared before Jack, breathless, anxious, unsure in an outfit I was considering wearing in the outside world, I twirled around and asked him if it was okay. Yes, he said. He always answered yes.

'Nah. It doesn't feel right,' I'd decide anyway, and run off to change again. Sometimes Jack would go down and wait in the car and rev the engine. I could smell the fumes wafting upstairs and it made me even more frenzied and hopeless. 'You know I can't walk out the door until I feel right,' I'd tell him when I finally got in the car and slammed the car door shut.

Sometimes I would have a mini breakdown, a mild panic would result in tears because I couldn't get the outfit right, and he would come back upstairs and try to calm me down, lay me on the bed like a delicate nightgown and say my name to me over and over until I settled. Ever since the doctor had brought it to my attention a couple of years earlier, I understood I had a tendency to spiral into a crippling anxiety. But Jack provided the soothing reassurance that staring at my dress hem used to give me. Now I relied on him being there when I needed him, to tell me it was all okay.

I was still performing spoken word in the band with Beck and Pete. We were playing gigs every couple of weeks, at bars and art openings and house parties. My outfit panic was always the worst on those nights. I was going to be up on a stage, with people watching. More than usual, it seemed vital that I felt right.

One night before a gig I was going through my dresses and my fingers caught on to the thick, botanical lace of a dress I'd never worn before. It had been Mum's and I'd seen Xanthe wear it; it had started out cream, but she had dyed it in tea to age it, like a child making a treasure map.

I pulled the lace dress on; its stiff form felt unusually fitted on my body, which was used to flowy things. But the sleeves were too tight and I had trouble pushing my arms through. With my movement restricted I struggled with the zip, and suddenly the Japanese dressing frame, which had been wobbling, crashed down on me and took me with it to the ground. I was trapped underneath a pile of dresses.

Jack heard the crash and the shriek and came running from the other room. When he saw me he started laughing, and I did too. As he helped me up we invented newspaper headlines: *Woman buried alive by her own clothes! Dress massacre! Fashion kills!*

Later that night, on stage, the restrictive sleeves were stopping me from freely flailing my arms and dancing, so I stopped caring. A drunken amputation will be fun, I thought. It's only fabric anyway and why does it matter. I tore a big rip in it like a movie ticket.

Sobering up on the drive home with Jack afterwards, I realised how wrecked the dress was. 'But it's Mum's!' I protested. I looked to him for answers but he had none. It seemed to me to be his fault; he should have stopped me from tearing it. We drove home in silence, and even though it was after midnight Jack closed the door to his study when he got home. I heard the tap-tapping of typing, an assignment that he was trying to finish.

I walked alone into our bedroom, where all the dresses still lay on the floor. My sleeve was flapping limply, torn under my arm and hanging by a few threads on the shoulder. I decided to make a pot of tea, take Jack a cup, a peace offering. I took down the tea set and when the water was boiled I watched mesmerised as the rich amber colour poured into the cup like sunshine. They really were tiny teacups.

I reached up again to the shelf where the matching sugar-bowl was kept, and my dangling sleeve swept the brimming teacup onto my bare thigh. The tea sizzled and burnt into the skin in seconds.

My scream was high-pitched and blood-curdling. Jack came running in to find me on the floor again, and this time there was no lightness or laughter. We sped to the hospital as the sun rose and there I was attended to and given pain-killers. Jack stayed home to look after me, carried the TV into our bedroom, brought me food. He picked up the discarded dress and folded it gently over the top of his hanger. I could feel the burn, covered with a firm gauze, emitting heat from my thigh, and even though the painkillers were working, I found that I was bawling anyway.

Summer came. How humid those Brisbane days were; the temperature frequently got up to forty degrees. It made me so tired all the time. Perhaps Morroville didn't really mean

Tomorrow Town; maybe it meant Morning Town. Because mornings were good. I woke up happy beside Jack until the day wore on and I'd get sadder and sadder until night came with these explosions of grief. I was always mad at him, and immediately afterwards, always sorry. Anger and sorrow coming one after the other like a two-step dance move. I kept having sputters of tears, a motor revving but not going anywhere. I'd perk up as twilight cooled the air and try to venture out onto the street, watch the dogs being walked. But I felt weighed down. The night I arrived to work already crying, my boss sent me straight back home. I knew there was something wrong with me but I couldn't work out what.

I dropped down into the sadness as if there was a cavern just waiting for me, a pre-existing mould that was dark, where I set like stone, a Lorelei-shaped hole I fitted perfectly into. I kept trying to understand it but the feeling had no source and no direction. It had come from nowhere, was going nowhere. I lay on the bed with Jack, both of us silent, my arm a bridge across his skinny bare chest. My breaths turned into sighs and the sighs became more frequent; I started hearing my mum in them.

I had memories of Mum seeming disenchanted in her home life, raising four kids, but she seemed to brush it off or otherwise find a way to deal with it. One way seemed to be by cooking exquisite and creative meals. I decided to try to re-enact the dinner parties she used to host. I created a guest list and invited new and interesting people I had met at the arts festival I volunteered at. The day of the dinner, I called my mum to get her recipe for chocolate mousse but started crying into the phone instead. She didn't know how to handle it. My being upset made her upset. 'Talk to your father,' she said huskily, and handed the phone over to him.

The maps my parents made for us were vague with only a destination in mind—they wanted us to be the cartographers, to fill in the empty oblong of space ourselves. But I wished they could just tell me what to do and where to go. I felt so lost. I wanted them to have answers.

'No wonder you're depressed,' Dad said, and him saying it out loud, that one word, unlocked something in me, gave me a feeling of sudden relief. It was the answer to a riddle I didn't know I was trying to solve. I was depressed. That was it. 'You've just done a creative writing degree and you have no future,' Dad said matter-of-factly. 'Of course you feel hopeless. Come back home and we'll build a shack for you to write in.' The offer made me cry even more. I couldn't run home to my parents—I was a grown-up. I couldn't leave my life with Jack. I told him I had to go, and put down the phone.

That night at the dinner party everyone smoked inside and we ate in the living room, which we hardly ever used.

My soup was burnt and the mousse didn't work out, but no one cared except me.

The next day, my sister Analiese came to visit. She'd recently given birth to a baby girl so porcelain and precious, so beautiful and smiley and cuddly, simultaneously miniature and yet enormous, lips like the crumpled pale petals of a poppy reaching out from its pod. Whenever I saw her I wanted her so badly. I could feel the gnawing hole inside me. I could now identify the something that could fill up the space. The idea consumed me; instead of writing poems on the backs of ticket stubs I wrote baby names, tearing them up before anyone came by. One night after a tedious double shift, I was feeling brave and asked Jack if we could have a baby. 'We're not ready for that!' he said. But seeing my desperation and sorrow, he added, 'If you can give me a good reason then we will.' All I could think of was, 'I just want one.' He shook his head. He seemed as sad about it as I was.

I was working six days a week. Jack was doing his exams and we didn't see each other much, so I got him free movie tickets whenever I could so we could at least be in the same building. On my breaks I snuck into the theatre and held his hand, watching scenes I'd already seen hundreds of times before. I'd take a torch to check the cinema, walk down the aisle, checking the exits. Sit back down next to him and make him laugh with horror-movie faces, the torch like a bouquet lighting up my face. Like I was trying to scare him.

One night I woke up and saw a strange woman in our bedroom. She was standing over us at the foot of the bed where we lay naked under the sheet. The windows were wide open because of the heat. The soft breeze was wishing the curtain into an ocean. Everything dark. I pushed myself up onto my elbow, squinting, trying to make sense of it; in our dim, crowded bedroom, the cloaked figure looked like one of our wardrobes come to life.

'Can I help you, please?' I instinctively switched on my award-winning customer service mode. She was a hunched, bulky figure; she was picking up things on our dresser, touching our clothes.

Jack bolted awake. He saw the woman. 'What do you want?' he said, his voice hoarse.

'I just need a lift,' she mumbled, adding that she needed to get to West End.

'We're already here,' Jack said, confused. 'We're already in West End.'

'Oh,' she said. She turned around and shuffled out of the room. Jack and I sat for a minute, paralysed, confused, in the dark, and then we sprang to life. Jack wrapped a towel around his waist and I threw on my dressing gown. We ran through the apartment, flicking on all the light switches, checking the heavy front door, then racing back to my office, the sunroom, which was dark. The woman had vanished. I pushed on the back door to see if it was unlocked like I did at the cinema, and there was the escape. The door led out to the perilous and wonky staircase she must have entered and left by.

Jack lit a cigarette, I made a cup of tea and we sat in the electric-brightness, staring at each other. Talking it over. Repeating what happened. 'She must have been here before, she must have known the previous tenants.' This made sense, we thought. But later, when we tried to explain it to friends, there was still a gap, an emptiness in the story. This disoriented woman echoed back a lost part of me. Had she once lived here with her boyfriend too? I wondered how she'd got to where she was now.

It was the end of the year and my sister Xanthe was getting married on an island off North Queensland. Neither Jack nor I had much money but I'd been saving and paid for his airfare. It was the first time he'd ever been on a plane.

The wedding was on the beach and we were all barefoot and dressed up. Xanthe looked like one of her wedding flowers, long, sleek and swirly in her white dress. Jack was dapper in his navy-blue suit, and when Analiese gave us her baby daughter to hold he tickled her and made silly faces at her to make her laugh.

We all sat down for dinner under the stars, and to listen to the wedding speeches. My dad and brother Lachy were allergic to seafood, but for some reckless reason Lachy decided to eat some crab anyway. Straight away he started turning blue. The speeches continued even as we called an ambulance, and in a split-second decision I travelled with him in the back of the emergency vehicle to the tiny hospital so that Mum and Dad wouldn't have to leave the wedding. Lachy was put on oxygen and gradually came back to life.

I sat with him, listening to the heavy up-down of his breathing, reassured at last that he was going to be okay. I had no phone and no way to contact Jack. He would be back there with my family, no doubt feeling awkward. Then, out of nowhere, he appeared. He had cycled over on the hotel bicycle without knowing where he was going, and when he arrived there were sweat marks soaking the underarms of his jacket. Lachy was still woozy so the three of us sat there, laughing about how annoyed Xanthe would be that her brother had upstaged her wedding. We missed the entire reception, so Jack and I made up the speeches we were missing to entertain Lachy while he waited to be given the all-clear so that he could leave.

On our way back from the hospital in a cab, I felt bad again. It was the time of the evening I usually felt numb, overcome with a sense of sadness. Under the pale blue hotel sheets, I asked Jack again in a whisper if we could have a baby. Even as I said it, I felt like a crazy woman, bewildered and lost and with no explanation of how I had got to this place, just knowing that this was where I found myself. Jack didn't answer, he just sighed and reached his arm across me like a bridge.

Back in Brisbane, we caught the train from the airport and were walking home along Vulture Street, the same street I had hauled the Japanese dressing frame along a year earlier. Jack walked in front of me, dragging our two suitcases behind him, and I called out to him that I was leaving.

When he spun around I tearfully asked, 'Is it okay?' and I knew that he would say yes. He always said yes, but still, it made me cry when I heard him shout it above the traffic. He could have asked me why it had taken so long for me to do it, why I had wasted all my savings flying him up to the wedding, but he didn't. He just turned around and kept walking.

We both knew how long it took me to get ready; we both knew I couldn't walk out the door until I felt right.

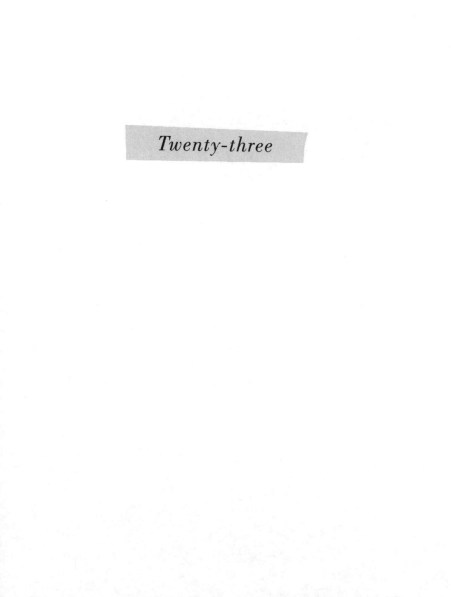

Twenty-three

The move to Melbourne from any other city in Australia makes you feel like a pioneer, one of those dusty and determined characters out of an American history novel trudging west to seek a land of gold and dreams. But here the goldfields are south, and the weather becomes colder, not hotter, and the people get more pale and shivery because of the nearness to Antarctica and the amount of coffee drunk.

It's a city founded by a guy called Batman, and laid out on a grid like a comic strip. There are plaques scattered throughout the town centre so when you look down the street you can compare it with how it looked a hundred years ago. Always new places are opening up, run-down buildings sleekly entrepreneured: bars blooming out of ancient cracked factories, old warehouses converted into apartments. Everything seems built over something, everything here used to be something else.

You're told you can find treasure—the secret bars hidden down the alleyways, the tiny shops filled with precious curios, the art openings overflowing out onto the street. But the true gold that paves Melbourne's footpaths is the promise that you can be a writer, an artist, a musician, a performer there. People who move there want to be discovered, they want to make a mark.

It was late January when I arrived, bright and sunny. I stopped in a daze in the middle of the street to look up at the European buildings, at window details, at the sky for some indication of the weather forecast, I slowed down and disrupted the flow of traffic to inspect someone's outfit before they disappeared into the lunchtime crowd.

When I heaved open a tall door in the centre of the city and climbed up two flights of stairs, I was in my new home. It was a warehouse, a large open space with dusty windows directing limbs of sunlight on the wooden floorboards. Canvases huddled in corners with their backs to me, an exhausted piano was pushed against a wall. The bedrooms were divided by thin, makeshift walls that didn't reach the ceiling. Only one light switch controlled the fluorescents for the whole space, so clusters of old lamps were gathered in everyone's rooms to light the space up at night like a movie set. The kitchen was at the back of the building, and here a ladder leaned unsteadily along the wall up to another bedroom and the roof. In the poky bathroom, a coral-coloured shower cubicle like something from a Barbie house was tacked on a platform so you had to step up into it like a ritual. The air was steeped in turpentine and nicotine.

I'd first seen Reuben in a newspaper article when I was at high school, because he'd won an award, and years later when I worked at an arts festival I had opened a filing cabinet and there was his face again, boy-like and wizened at the same time, staring out from inside a manila folder. I don't know why but I remembered him. Perhaps because we were the same age, except he had a successful creative career. He lived two states away in a city I'd never been before, but it seemed like fate that we would meet, and when he came to the festival in Brisbane we did.

I had started sending him letters by post to Melbourne, the only way I knew how. He replied with emails like he was from the future and I wanted to be there too, where he was. So I sent him an email. I told him I was moving down. Did he know of any rooms for rent? He wrote back the next day. A room was available at his place. Everything was so instant. I could see the future.

Reuben's housemates were writers, artists, musicians. The night I arrived we bought bottles of wine and had a spontaneous reading aloud from our favourite books. There was Kafka and Celine, and I read from *Franny and Zooey*.

'All I know is I'm losing my mind,' I began. It was the part where Franny is telling her boyfriend why she quit the theatre. 'I'm just sick of ego, ego, ego. My own and everybody else's. I'm sick of everybody that wants to get somewhere, do something distinguished and all, be somebody interesting. It's disgusting—it is, it *is*. I don't care what anybody says.' Everyone clapped, and I curtsied.

Very quickly the place felt like a home, a family, all of us drawn to the kitchen every night as the kettle whistle called us to come together on the old couch for cups of tea in the cramped, windowless kitchen.

I started smoking, a way to inhale it all, to get even more out of the hours of sitting and talking. I immediately felt a part of this intimate, hospitable group of friends, but my gaze kept wandering back to Reuben. I loved to watch him talk. His speech always seemed ordered and arranged beforehand; it came out fully formed like poetry, the tatters of a childhood stutter beaten back in real time so when words were repeated they came across as emphasis, conviction. His hands were nimble narrators. If they weren't collaborating with him on a story he kept them clasped together on his lap like a little boy in a school photo, an ankle jiggling on his opposite knee, but every now and then one of his hands would escape and dart up behind his ear where there must have been a switch that turned on his laugh—a Cheshire cat chuckle—before the hand fled back and got wrapped protectively around by its twin like he was incubating a punch.

He exhumed stories from people like a rogue grave-digger, finding bodies you didn't know you'd even buried. He pulled them out of me too. We talked into the early morning, turning them over together to inspect the decay, and afterwards he lay them back down in their hole and patted the soil, knowing now the dirt would always be disturbed, fresh. In exchange he told me stories too, about growing up and his life in this city. He also told me about other women he'd known, anecdotes I thought were too intimate and private to share with someone he barely knew, but his openness made me feel closer to him.

My favourite discussions were always about the creative working process. 'Do you think you have to like what you make?' I asked him one night. 'I mean, in terms of what you create, like your writings or drawings or compositions or whatever?'

He stared at me intently. 'Do you?'

'I do but I don't. I mean, I do think it's important, but I never do like anything I do!'

He considered it a moment. 'Yeah, I do think you need to like it, but that satisfaction can be transient.' He ashed his cigarette into an empty chip packet. 'I usually get the most intense joy from the actual doing,' he added, 'so I suppose no matter whether I like a finished piece or not, the drive will always be there to continue making things.' He handed me his lighter and I smiled, and lit another cigarette.

I'd been living there for a couple of weeks when one of our housemates, a painter called Lucas, noticed that my clothes were still packed up in the massive purple suitcase I'd hauled down with me. 'You have to hang them up, put them on show, exhibit them,' he told me. He started tapping on the walls of my bedroom until he found the supporting struts, and took out a biro and made some marks on the wall. On the back of an envelope he sketched his wardrobe design, and we walked together to the hardware store where he picked out brackets and long pieces of dowel. We carried them home together, the poles hitting things as we walked, awkward shapes to get through our narrow doorway.

The humming of the power drill turned my walls into hangers. Instead of sidling up alongside the walls, parallel, the hangers stuck out straight like two zombie arms, reaching right across the ocean of my bedroom. They were set high enough so that the longer dresses wouldn't trail on the floor. When at last they were all hung I had a room full of ghostly, floating women. The equals sign of dresses divided the room into two—an equator, separating sleep and work. I could swim through the dresses between worlds, the spheres of home and writing, of art and life. Just as we finished Reuben came home and peered into my room. He took hold of a long pink satin skirt by the hips and ran his hands down the shiny bones that rippled through the fabric, and I shivered.

That night we pulled each other into a dark corner and started kissing. 'You know I'm with Alice, right?' he said.

I didn't. I felt stupid. In all our conversations he hadn't mentioned it until now. We pulled away. The next day he knocked on my door and I opened it, shy and embarrassed in the daylight. I had lain awake all night. I hadn't been able to stop thinking of the time when I was eighteen and I wondered if I was in love with a woman. I'd walked around in a daze for a month, both anxious and exhilarated by the thought *What if I'm gay?* Both the fear and passion of that obsession had soon fizzled, but this was the same giddy–scary anticipation of discovering something unexpected I hadn't known about myself: *What if I'm a cheat? The 'other' woman?*

'So, about last night,' he said, and we laughed uncomfortably. 'We'll just be friends, right?' His tone was relaxed and jovial, and it reassured me. After all, we hadn't really done anything.

'Right,' I said, relieved that it was now clear, that I knew what the boundaries were. We smiled and shook hands.

After that, Alice was around the house more often. She was a beautiful artist: tall, smart and interesting. I got to know her and liked her. I found myself asking all about her, her family, wanting to know where she had travelled and what she thought about everything. I still liked Reuben a lot, but Alice's presence in the house acted as an amulet, protection so I wouldn't be with him.

During the week everyone in the house was busy working on songs and paintings and stories and films, but on weekends there was always a party. Sometimes other people would come over but mostly it would just be the housemates, our bodies strewn across someone's bedroom floor and forming one more layer on top of the ash-laden carpet, an eruption of wine and gin and drugs preserving us there and then. In Brisbane my friends and I had approached the taking of drugs as a family, setting up a mattress in someone's living room and settling in peacefully to drop acid or ecstasy and listen to records and jam and talk, and here I had found the same intimate togetherness. We didn't need the outside. A camera was pulled out and we posed in memento mori tableaux, cigarettes our chosen motif in place of skulls. I took a photo of Alice and Reuben, their heads pressed together like conjoined twins, cigarettes hanging out of their mouths and eyes closed.

One day Reuben was cleaning up and throwing out clothes, and asked me if I wanted any. I picked out a few things, including a baggy olive-striped cardigan. I had to roll the sleeves up, but wearing it made me feel close to him, embraced. It seemed like it was enough.

From the first day, Melbourne had made me want to write. My desk was a pale blue door I found in the stairwell, held up by two hip-high shelves from the hardware store. I wheeled an old office chair from Reuben's room into mine and started to type.

My dad had sent down my old massive computer, a big desktop PC that was carried up the stairs by a man with a clipboard and a cap. I started at last to write stories on it, permanent and plot-driven, not like the ones I had always scribbled on paper, so easy to tear up or misplace or throw out. Characters who were more like caricatures or comic-book heroes, scenes frozen and self-contained in their own boxes that went nowhere; I concentrated on the colours and the speech bubbles of a scene and tried to make each swatch as exciting and dramatic as possible. My women were churlish and childish and weighed down with jewellery and neuroses. They slunk around the house in slips, and were accompanied by the gentle tinkling of ice against the décolletage of a high-ball glass. There was always an impossible love affair, a love triangle, a melodrama, a gulf too impossible to be bridged, tacky and over-the-top like something out of *Dynasty*. I understood the appeal of those stories now; love had started to feel dramatic and intense and impossible, but also real.

One night I came home late and Lucas and Reuben were tearing about the house. Reuben was doing chin-ups on the beam in the hallway and Lucas batted on the drums. Reuben hung for as long as he could from the beam, hands shredding on the splintering baulk, while Lucas drummed and puffed and shouted incomprehensible anythings. They were in a crazy mood and I felt a surge of adrenaline when I walked into the room.

Lucas ran up and grabbed my bag and chucked it in my bedroom, took from me the bottles of red wine I had brought home, and corralled us all into the kitchen. Pouring the wine into mugs, he instructed us to paint the kitchen walls, spray them, do anything. 'Here're some brushes,' he cried out. 'You can use this paint and this one, but not this because I need it to finish off that canvas in my room.'

And away we went, screaming, chanting, singing. I was painting little girly circles, swirling different colours, repeating the pattern over and over. Lucas worked on a patch of space he was making thick and blue, and Reuben was spraypainting words all over the wall, words like MONDAY and TUESDAY and FUCK. He tore the toaster from the wall, so its cord dangled tail-like and forlorn, and all of a sudden he threw it against the wall. Lucas, grinning, picked it up and threw it again and this time it burst completely, scattering little robot intestines across the floor. Reuben then took a plate, just a side plate, something that didn't match anything anyway, and chucked it against the wall too.

I was squealing and sheltering my head in my arms each time it happened. 'What are you guys doing? We'll have nothing left!' At that, Reuben picked up a dinner plate, a discus, and flung it against the wall so it became undone like shoelaces, decorating the room with long, spinning, paisley shards.

I let out a scream and picked up a glass and threw it so the smash bounced back at me. My hands instinctively flew up to protect my face. The boys howled with happiness. Swept up in their energy I then flung a sweet chilli sauce bottle at the wall and when it hit it sounded like a skull cracking on pavement, leaving polka dots of stickiness that swiftly divided and subdivided on every surface like a disease.

We threw plates at the wall until there were no plates left, or glasses, or toaster, just three mismatched mugs spilling over with wine. Lucas leaned against the bench, panting heavily like he'd just won a sporting event. Reuben stood rolling a cigarette, smiling at what he was doing, working the tobacco beneath his fingers as if he was playing Nintendo, then licking the paper. The match strike made him guffaw as he lit the cigarette hanging out of his mouth, and he turned to us and grinned.

His teeth and lips were black-stained, and I burst out laughing. 'What's wrong?' he asked, and when I told him, he said, 'Look at yourself!' I went to the toilet and saw in the mirror that mine were purply black too. We were exactly the same. When I came back out Lucas had fallen asleep on the couch. Reuben and I were wide awake, and crept away to be together.

For weeks we found glass everywhere. We had to be careful now in that house. We couldn't even walk without cutting ourselves. A regular rhythm started. At night the whole household stayed awake until early morning, playing music and talking and watching movies, until one by one everyone went to bed, except for Reuben and me. I admired his manic working attitude; he was most productive during the early hours of the morning, making headway on some interesting new project which impressed me but which he would shrug off as everyday. Sometimes just sitting in the same room while he worked was enough, and I would slip into the rhythm of his typing and fill my own notebook quickly as well. Eventually he might invite me to watch another movie with him or dig through the old magazines and books that lined the shelves of his room. Or we would simply just stay up talking until the soft scratches of our voices abraded the night, until a pale blue glow invaded the room and started reassembling the blobbish shapes around us into furniture. That's when the lamps began to squirm conspicuously and it was time for me to kiss the deep bed of his brambly cheek. This was the moment he would take my hands as though they were his own, and sometimes we would say goodnight and sometimes we would say goodnight for hours.

As I lived it I wrote it, trying to understand how I felt so empty and yet so full. The words in my diaries seemed proof of what happened. But even the 'I' who was wrangling the pen, holding it tremulously like a divining rod over my diary and forcing it back on course any time it tried to make excuses for what I was doing, didn't know whether it was even real. Whether it was even me. We told each other we loved each other. I knew there were rules, that he was someone else's boyfriend, and every time we were together we'd promise it was a one-off. Sometimes we stayed away from each other for days, sometimes weeks, but we always found our way back.

Soon, though, he started spending more time away and I would only see him every few days. The place felt empty when he was gone and I'd long for him to come home. Then when he did we'd fall into each other again, always followed by a meek knock on the door the next day where he'd smile shyly and sheepishly and we'd both promise it wouldn't happen again.

The decisive feeling stayed while he was away, and in the light of the day it didn't hurt so much. But at night, without his presence in the house, the comforting tap-tap coming from his computer in the room next door, I barely slept. There was so much going on in my mind—my thoughts pestered me and stories went round and round my head, a mixture of the fiction I was writing and the real life I was living.

One night I woke in the early hours of the morning and my whole body was numb. I couldn't move; my legs had gone dead. When I could eventually stand I pulled on the olive cardigan and went out to the kitchen to get a glass of water. I walked in on them on the couch, Alice's long body wrapped around his. They moved apart quickly.

'Sorry,' I said.

'That cardigan was mine,' Alice said, sitting up. 'Well, my grandma's actually.'

'Seriously?' I looked at Reuben. 'Reuben gave it to me. Do you want it back? You can have it back.'

'No, it's fine. Keep it. I didn't want it anymore.'

I mixed bleach and peroxide together, guessing the measure-ments and wrapping my hands in plastic supermarket bags to slather the paste over my head, leaving it on until the tingling burn on my scalp was too much. Marking myself out from Alice, whose hair was long and shining and auburn.

When I had moved down I'd been able to get a transfer to a cinema in Melbourne, and I worked there a few days a week. I stumbled sleep-deprived to my shifts each morning. I'd try to go and see as many films as I could, measure the size of the stories on the screen with what was happening outside in my life, finding that the characters in my real life were bigger. More interesting. 'Hey Blondie!' I'd be yelled at along Russell Street in my work uniform during the day, dealers beckoning to me to follow them into a game arcade, and as I shrugged them off I wondered how they knew about the darkness inside me, how they had recognised it. I began to get paranoid. Scared of being caught. But in the dim cinema I felt brave enough to take on the city, dare it to stop me. I deserved this. The love, the largeness, the drama, and whatever else came with it. I didn't feel like the baddie. I felt like the hero: I had found love. I had got it. I was at my best when I was with Reuben. My thoughts were clearer and more interesting; I knew who I was when I was with him. Lately, though, he'd been getting irritable. He would come to me and tell me he and Alice had broken up and then a few days later inform me they were back together again. He'd get impatient about the simplest things.

'Do you want to get some wine?' he asked one night when he got home.

'I'm not sure,' I hesitated. 'I have to work in the morning—'

'It's either yes or no, Lorelei,' he interrupted. 'You can't be so vague. You have to decide.'

I was startled by the forceful insistence of his voice. I'd become so accustomed to accepting contradictions and complexities and shades of grey—our entire relationship was based on prevarication. And I'd become comfortable with not needing to decide whether I was good or bad or right or wrong with him. We could exist one way in the murky night and another when daylight came. I said no to the wine and without another word he slipped out of the house, and I knew he wouldn't be home again soon.

Some of my friends from Brisbane moved down. I arranged to meet up with them nearby at one of the city bars. They wanted to come up and see the crazy Melbourne warehouse I lived in. I made excuses. 'We're shooting a film,' I told them. I didn't want other people inside my world, I didn't want them to burst it. I didn't want to share it; but I also didn't want to see it reflected through other people's eyes, in case they showed me how insane it actually was.

As the months got colder I asked Mum to send down a box of my winter clothes that I'd left at home. They were clothes you never needed in the Brisbane climate: my great-grandmother's thick ivy green cardigan, with a missing button. A pink-and-grey Chanel jacket, an eighties original, that I had inherited from Xanthe; a blue, woollen two-piece suit. I waited for the package but it never arrived. The only things that came by post were letters from Jack, Brisbane to Melbourne every week. Big yellow envelopes filled with stuff. Jack used any paper he could find to write on; sometimes he typed it up on our old typewriter, other times he scrawled in blue biro. He enclosed records or books or Polaroids. Distance seemed to bring us closer, it became easier to confide in him. When we had been together I'd expected him to know what I was thinking and feeling, without saying it out loud; I communicated with a semaphore of shifting eye contact and shrugs and grimaces. The letters now made everything clear. I told Jack that I was in love with Reuben, and that I missed him, Jack, too. Both were true. He didn't judge me for having so many feelings at once. He said he missed me as well.

I hadn't seen Reuben in a few days when Mum phoned, urging me to go to the post office and ask about the missing package. That day, just leaving the house seemed like an epic undertaking. I picked out a dress that would make me feel good: a musk stick, the colour a sunset or a bruise starts out at, a pink destined to go purplish and then finally turn black. It had looked shapeless and baggy on the hanger when I'd bought it, but the woman in me emerged when I slid it on. In it, I instantly had shape, form. A purpose. I zipped it up. Put my hands in the pockets. It was eighties style and the tag said

Suzanne Grae; mass-produced, replaceable, a dime a dozen, like me, just like every other young girl who'd moved to the big smoke. The cross-my-heart front of the dress made me happy but when I caught sight of myself in a shop window as I walked by, I could see that my underwear line was showing. I became self-conscious. I was sure everyone could see through me.

I strode to the post office on Elizabeth Street. They couldn't tell me anything. They couldn't say if my package had been delivered or if it had even arrived. I asked the café below us, the hairdresser, the 7-Eleven. Maybe they'd received it by mistake. For the first time since I moved in, I became conscious of living in a big city. People existed, did things, thought about other subjects besides Reuben. Walking, following the grid of the city, taking in its grey blocks, I reflected on all the things he taught me and showed me, the movies, the books, the music, the people. The perfect cocoons of the stories he told, how they were complete and textured and full of something living that connected with me so truthfully. I was walking with my head down and without any warning I felt a striking force heave into me. I was thrown to the ground. An old woman pushed by me and continued waddling down the street, looking back with fury in her eyes, swearing at me.

'You're crazy, you bitch!' she screamed at me.

'*You're* crazy!' I yelled back from the footpath.

'Crazy bitch! Crazy bitch!' she taunted as she picked up her pace and disappeared down the street. People were rushing to help. My bag had been thrown and my hands were prickled and punctured by the concrete. 'That woman is crazy!' I told the people who rushed up—a man, an elderly woman, both nodding, witnesses. Dazed, the dress hugging my legs closed, I felt my knees were bloodied, a bruise swelling. The strangers picked me up by the armpits but when I was standing I stepped away from them. I hugged my bag to my chest and started moving down Swanston Street, tears welling, wondering what I had done. She was the crazy one, not me. The house was empty when I got home, and that's when I felt my dress had torn, the split at the back had ripped when I fell, like the tail of a mermaid transformed sharply and cruelly into legs.

Our hot water had been shut off weeks earlier because we hadn't paid the bill, so I had to go to the city baths to get clean, wearing an aqua one-piece of my mum's with a frilled V-neck. I did laps in the heated pool, the flounces ruffled gently as I swam and everything was silent as the water cut over me. Underwater I could hear myself again, heart beating calm, the quietude of chlorine, of salt, of an element, a mineral other than himself inside me and on me and above and around me. Swimming with my body that kicked like an instinct. But when I broke the surface I was still drowning. I wanted him to choose me and not choose me.

When I got my period it was weeks late but everything was topsy-turvy, because I was drinking and smoking and forgetting to take my pill. The period cramps hurt so much I had to call in sick at work and stay in bed all day, and I couldn't shake the thought that I might have been pregnant and now I wasn't anymore. And later, when the night fell blue-black, I told Reuben, in a scene performed by the two worst actors in a bad soap opera; I told him like I told him everything, our cigarettes like headlights, both staring straight ahead on the couch, dialogue stilted.

He said gravely, I'm sorry to hear that, like a relative had just died, which was appropriate because maybe one had. But then maybe one hadn't. I wasn't sure, I kept telling him, it might have been nothing, I was now saying it to myself except it was out loud, it might just have been a really heavy period. For once he wasn't trying to dig deeper, he wasn't asking me questions but I kept answering them anyway.

When he finally spoke it was to ask why wasn't I angry with him; he said that I should hate him, that I should punch him. I stood up and said I'm the baddie, not you, and even though I swayed there pale and mute like a Robert Palmer girl, I screwed my fist up tightly in a static punch and pressed it into my eye socket instead, trying to get back that lucky feeling, the grateful feeling, the one I usually had when he was with me instead of anyone else.

And a while later, maybe weeks or a whole month, after Reuben had disappeared again for a long time and the anti-depressants that the free community doctor had given me had kicked in, after the hallucinations that projected blobby wombats the size of small cars into the room had calmed down, after I'd stood trembling for an hour on the corner of La Trobe Street before finally deciding not to step out in front of a truck, after I hadn't pressed quite hard enough with the Stanley knife to stop myself from being alive, after a spate of panic attacks had taught me what it's like to feel as if you're watching yourself die in slow motion, after all that, Reuben came back one night and we had a big party.

Everything was like before. We tumbled back into each other's arms, crawling away only in the early morning to go to sleep in our separate beds. When I woke up late in the afternoon to a knock on my bedroom door I instantly knew it wouldn't be him, that it would be Alice instead. Because for so long I had just wanted to be discovered and the night before I had finally made my mark: I had left a hickey on his neck, a gravelly engraving with my teeth.

I opened the door and she was white like porcelain, cold and still with the shock and hurt of her discovery, and I stood against the frame of the doorway facing her, the olive threads of her grandmother's baggy knitted cardigan unravelling around me. I wish she'd slapped my face, I wish she'd shouted or said something sarcastic and wry or angry, but she just stood in the hallway, the glossy perimeters of the bar it was to become years later hovering there, waiting for us to end it, for it to all come crashing around us so something else could be built—shelves of bottles and shining faucets and atmospheric lighting and people who weren't us.

I was drained of all desire for deception, so when she asked I told her the truth, and the truth when I heard it out loud wasn't as melodramatic as I had imagined in my head for all these months. There was no screaming or face slapping. The truth was a short conversation, quiet and civil and completely awful.

She went to leave but then stopped. Turning and looking me straight in the eyes she asked me if I loved him. I blurted out, 'I don't know,' and instantly felt ashamed at lying about the only thing I had known to be true this entire time, a woeful effort to protect myself and downplay the intensity of what had happened. But as she walked away I realised that the 'yes' that had been pulsing recklessly through my blood for so many months had disappeared. 'I don't know' had become true now.

I could hear the hurried activity of the city two floors down, people rushing home from their offices as the wind turned the winter sunshine into mayhem. The trams shuddered, and after the door slammed once, I heard another set of footsteps thump past my door and it slammed again, then I knew I was really alone. I fell down on the blue couch and tried to stop the room from swaying. I pulled the cardigan close around me and even though I understood that now she got to hurt the most, that those were the rules, I had already broken so many that it didn't seem to matter anymore.

Twenty-four

My hair was damp and wrapped in an old towel. Earlier that morning, I had cut off a blonde strand to keep, like I was my own sweetheart, and dyed the rest black. I was back in Buderim at my parents' house for Christmas, and for my best friend Katherine's wedding. She was on her way over to deliver my bridesmaid dress. Since I'd been back I had tried to distract myself, read books, watch films, but the risk was that in trying to forget Reuben I would accidentally remember him: a word or turn of phrase, a particular actor, a piece of music, my thoughts like a colony of insects programmed to find their way back to him. I had been excited for Kat's wedding all year, but now I felt so tired. All I wanted to do was sleep forever.

When I opened the cupboard to look for something to wear besides my pyjamas, shining back at me in its clear protective bag was the yellow dress I had worn to my school ball when

I was sixteen. The ball replaced the debutante that had, just as I reached the right age to be a part of it, been deemed too politically incorrect for the times and banned. No more girls in white. At sixteen I couldn't agree more that 'presenting' women to society made no sense, but still, I wanted to wear a white dress like my sisters had done. It seemed so unfair that I couldn't. My friend Jemima had given me some yellow satin bed sheets that her parents didn't want anymore—'too slippery to sleep on'—and I asked Mum if she could make me a dress out of them, in the same style as the black-and-white ball gown Audrey Hepburn wears in *Sabrina* after she comes back from Paris, transformed.

Taking it out of the wardrobe now, the dress made me feel even sadder. Unworn since that night, the tangerine tulle underskirt flounced out eagerly. Mum always said how challenging it had been to sew because the satin was so slippery. As I zipped it up I remembered the tickly feeling of her hands, measuring and pinning the fabric to my shape, the sound of her dressmaking scissors creaking along the fabric, the bottom jaw sailing across the big dining table where she worked every night after the dinner plates were cleared. I'd loved the dress and felt glamorous in it. Now, I stepped back into it like into another time.

It was the year before I went to Turkey. There was a framed photo of me on the mantelpiece wearing the dress alongside pictures of my two sisters in their white deb dresses. My little niece had pointed to it and cried out, 'Belle!' when she saw it. She meant Belle from Disney's *Beauty and the Beast*. I hadn't made that connection myself at the time, but now I wondered if that was the impression I gave. At sixteen, did I consider myself to be some sort of fairytale princess? It seemed weird. I had never been brought up to believe in that, to expect a man would save me. My mum had drummed into us that education was more important than marriage. And in the Broadway shows and old movies I'd always loved, the women were dramatic and feisty, not drips who sat around waiting for a man. But seeing the photograph of me sitting against the sapphire-blue backdrop, my hair done up in a *Gone with the Wind* style, I did look frothy and flouncy, as if I might believe in a prince coming to save me. The idea of that now appalled me.

'Oh my god, Lorelei—your hair!' yelped Kat as she walked in. We both burst into tears. She sat on the edge of my bed and we clung to each other for a few moments.

'I remember this dress,' she said, patting the satin of the skirt like it was a pet. 'Wasn't that ball ridiculous. Do you remember how I wore the same dress as someone's mum?'

We laughed. Someone's *mum*!

'And I was wearing Jemima's parents' bedsheets!'

'What *were* we!'

Kat and I had met when we were eight years old and instantly decided to love each other. Back then she wore a corrective eye patch, like a big, circular bandaid, and glasses over the top. I had never seen anyone who looked like that. Moreover, she wasn't even self-conscious about it so she didn't get teased. Her hair was wavy and pure white-blonde, not like mine, which straggled greasily past my shoulders and was a non-descript porridge colour. We were inseparable. Our lives were all about sleepovers, play dates, about just another ten minutes in the pool and 'Can't you pick me up an hour later, Mum?' In grade four the teacher separated us for the whole year because we giggled too much but we clambered back to each other at every break, killing each other with the jokes we made up and grabbing hold of the other's familiar warm hand whenever we walked anywhere. The small knobbly wart on the inside of her thumb undisgusting to me because it was hers.

We were known as Kit Kat and Lolly and we got matching boys' haircuts. I'd always get a nosebleed on the trampoline, in the pool, on the pillowcase, and Kat would squeal, 'Lorelei! Not again!' But she was used to it and didn't actually care. She had two older brothers and a younger sister and I had two older sisters and a younger brother. Our aim in life was to get any of them or all of them to marry each other so we could be proper sisters forever.

Then, in our final year of primary school, Katherine met Louisa. They became best friends and I was devastated. It was the summer before high school and I missed her like crazy. I tried not to think about Kit Kat and Louisa having so much fun, riding Louisa's horses and going rollerskating. At high school, Kat was put in a different class and we drifted apart even more. We both made new friends, but remained in each other's orbit. At the start of Year 12 we took French classes together outside of school, and that's when I found out she was going on a student exchange and realised I had to go too. Kat, who had been struck by the good-lookingness of a Canadian football team who had toured our school, had chosen to spend a year in Canada. Amid our preparations for leaving, we came back together, organising a joint bon-voyage party and making invitations fashioned as fake passports. Everyone had to dress up in red and white, the colours of our host countries' flags. At the party we spun each other around to 'Dancing Queen' and it felt like ABBA was singing just to us because we were young and sweet and only seventeen too.

The night I arrived in Istanbul I lay down on my new double bed, in my neat and ordered room that was like a teenager's bedroom in an American sitcom, and picked up the pale pink telephone. The maids brought in a bowl of fresh fruit—peaches, pears and plums—and I admired the view out my window across the rose garden as I phoned home. My dad answered and I immediately started gushing about The Palace, but he interrupted me saying he had bad news. Kat's eldest brother had been killed in a work accident. It was one week before she was due to fly to Canada. That night I curled up, cold and lonely, even though it was summer and I had a TV in my room and a swimming pool in the living room. I wanted to be with Kat and her family, who were like my second one.

She still decided to go on her student exchange, delaying it only to attend the funeral. She was sent to live with an impersonal French–Canadian host family in the sub-zero remote suburbs of Quebec. We wrote to each other, phoned each other, both homesick. Kat described how her host family had four TVs, one for each member of the family, and after dinner they all went to their own rooms to watch them separately.

We had delayed our Year 12 in order to do the exchange, and when we came home to Australia we both tried our best to fit back in for our final year of high school. I felt changed. I wanted to fit in with the girls who knew about music and movies and fashion, and Kat became really religious. It wasn't the youth-groupy lite religion we had both grown up with—singing in Christmas pageants and occasionally going to Sunday school. This religion was a full-time job. At first it didn't seem too strange, an understandable response to losing

her brother, but she quickly threw herself into it until everything she did seemed connected in some way to the church.
And so, while I was in my first year of university in Brisbane,
bingeing on *Buffy* and cultivating crushes on my tutors, she
was organising fundraising ventures and volunteering at
a mission that helped underprivileged youth. When I was
working at the cinema, spending all my money on records,
she worked in the office of the church as a pastor's assistant,
earning less than five dollars an hour. Then a couple of years
later, when she'd started going to Bible college to train to be
a pastor, she called me to say she had met Phillip. He was
literally the son of a preacher man. She asked if I'd be her
bridesmaid and I accepted straight away. I knew she now had
lots of new friends, and it was an honour. I felt close to her
again. Like I was her best friend again.

In my parents' spare room wearing the yellow dress, I
suddenly wanted Kat to know everything. About the past year,
about Reuben, my heartache, how terrible love was. I sat up
and, in sputtered gulps, told her, hoping my parents wouldn't
overhear this version of the story, the more traumatic one I'd
protected them from. She clasped my hands and listened. Kat
always had the most optimistic and upbeat response to the
very worst situations. I was imagining she'd say something
like: 'Let it make you, not break you! You can make a choice
about how to deal with it!' But with tears in her eyes she told

me God could help me if I asked Him. I looked away, embarrassed, and tried to turn the conversation around. I told her, thank you, it's okay, I feel so much better now. But the gulf between us had opened up again. She hugged me over the slippery yellow sheets I was wearing, and I froze up in her arms, wondering how she could be so sure of things when I was unsure of everything.

Before Kat left, she hung the bridesmaid dress up in the cupboard. I lay back and looked at it, pearly pink satin, strapless and fitted, unflattering on me, picked out by someone who didn't know me anymore. I felt like I had been away a really long time.

I turned the DVD back on. The summer heat pressed at the flyscreen over the window and I sat watching *Who's Afraid of Virginia Woolf?* wondering why anyone got married, but especially women and especially women my age, in their twenties. Sure, I had convinced myself I wanted to marry Jack a couple of years earlier, but that was because I couldn't think of anything else to do with my life. I had been desperate, trying to fill the hole, the yawning emptiness that engulfed me. That, and I knew in the back of my mind Jack was too smart to say yes.

But now, I saw it clearly. When women got married they suddenly walked taller. Their wedding rings shone like swords that transformed them, like knights in medieval times. They obtained a certainty, a confidence. Where did they learn to do that? How can people be tricked into feeling that secure, that safe? I'd seen it in my sisters when they were married, and in other girls from my school. Marriage changed them; they seemed like proper people.

I thought about my sister Analiese, the first one in our family to get married. The wedding was in our garden, which was overgrown and wild, but Mum and Dad had filled in the holes the echidnas had dug in the lawn and created a clearing where Analiese's friends sang 'Hallelujah'. A fountain was installed, the pond filled with goldfish that would be eaten by toads shortly after the wedding. Mum made our bridesmaid dresses—simple, short sleeveless shifts in white—and on our feet we wore Doc Martens with white satin ribbons threaded through the eyelets. Analiese wore a pale blue wedding dress, her long blonde hair hanging in tousled curls. She was nineteen and beautiful. To me, there was a sorrow in the air. Everyone was pretending to be okay, but whenever I turned a corner, walked into a room, someone would be crying. My little brother Lachy was gruff, mute, fourteen. My eldest sister Xanthe was typically loud and trying to keep things light, but her sandpapery remarks scraped against the tiled walls as the three of us girls got ready in the bathroom. I was hoping during the speeches that Dad would make a corny, uncharacteristic father-of-the-bride joke—'We're losing a daughter but gaining a bathroom!'—but he didn't, he just smiled and got on with it. Mum busied herself in the kitchen and acted cheerful. But earlier in the day when they walked their second daughter down the verandah, which had been transformed into a wedding aisle, they both had tears in their eyes. All parents cry at their kids' weddings, I remember thinking at the time—it's normal. But nothing in our family had been the same since.

I heard Mum calling me from the living room. Analiese's daughter was over and Mum needed me to look after her while she went out. I could hear my niece crying. I had babysat and been around toddlers long enough now to grumpily accept that children always get the attention: some do it by screaming their heads off, and I guess others do it by getting married. I snapped the movie off, ignoring the voice in my head that said, *And others do it by dyeing their hair black*, and huffed out into the living room.

Analiese announced we'd be having Christmas Day at her house, combining her husband's family and ours. She lived in the suburbs and I was dreading it. The day was sweltering hot and they didn't have a pool. Mum usually made me a special vegetarian meal, but this year the dish she made was left at home by accident and all I ended up eating was roast potatoes and watching as everyone cooed over my niece and baby nephew. Usually when I came home for Christmas I would noisily tell stories about the city, but this year I was too depressed to chime in. I was still on the antidepressants and they made me feel numb and apathetic. I retreated to the living room and sat in the lumpy brown beanbag in front of an electric fan. My nose was bleeding because I was allergic to Analiese's cat so I lay with my head tilted back to stem the blood and my eyes closed. The book Mum had got me for Christmas as a joke—*101 Things You Don't Need a Man For!*, a single woman's guide to fixing things around the house—was lying unopened beside me. I felt a foot nudge into me and it was my brother, Lachy, telling me to get up. He'd got the car keys off Dad; someone else would give them a lift home later. I almost hugged him, and we got out of there.

In the car, Lachy grunted. 'I feel so replaced.'

I looked at him, relieved that someone was thinking the same thing. 'I know!' I paused. 'But it's weird to be jealous of the grandkids. It doesn't seem right.'

He shrugged. 'Ever since they came along Mum and Dad just haven't been around. They're always focused on the grandkids. Everything is about them.'

I sighed. 'Yeah, but how can you compete with actual *babies*?' Neither of us had an answer.

Back at home Lachy retreated to his room and I went out by myself to sit on the rusty old swing set where Kat and I used to do gymnastics, twirling somersaults around the metal frame and other trapeze tricks. I used to come out here when I was twelve, where no one could hear me, to practise the Major-General's song from *The Pirates of Penzance*, a tongue-twisting, star-making song. Under the eucalypts I'd attach a paper moustache with sticky tape and practise bellowing out the song in my girlish baritone. I'd always wanted the part of Mabel, the pretty and sweet heroine, but Kat had deservedly got the role. 'Look, you're either Snow White or you're the Evil Queen,' Xanthe told me at the time, trying to console me. 'You're either the strong woman or the pretty heroine. Everyone knows that. You can't be both.' Two weeks before the show opened Kat gave her lead role away to another girl. She didn't want to stand out and preferred being in the chorus instead, one of the Major-General's many daughters, and she stood daintily up the back on a raised platform while I swept across the front of the stage in my fake moustache and got the laughs.

I tried to do a somersault on the swing-set frame, but on my first go I banged my head on the ground. I'd got too big for this.

The day before Kat's wedding, I dragged myself out of bed to get my eyelashes tinted at the appointed beauty salon. The other bridesmaids were already there when I arrived. They were getting spray tans as well but I politely said no. I lay behind a partition with my eyes closed, waiting for my eyelashes to dry and listening to the other bridesmaids' chatter. They were sweet girls from Kat's church. I listened to them talking about the wedding, about Kat, but it sounded like they were talking about someone else. I had been used to being the noisy, strong one in our relationship, the confident one, but here I could see Kat was a leader, someone with strong opinions and morals, who these girls admired and gushed over.

I was the last to arrive at Kat's parents' house the next day, where I'd spent so many weekend and summer sleepovers. The bride-to-be was nervous-vomiting when I arrived with the pale pink bridesmaid dress slung haphazardly over my arm. 'Thank goodness you're here, Lorelei. I need you,' she said, but she didn't really. She had everything organised.

When she washed her face and started putting on make-up, she grew calm and happy. She was doing exactly what she wanted to do. In her wedding dress that she had already planned to sell on eBay afterwards, she looked pretty and strong at the same time.

Next to the blonde and tanned bridesmaids waiting at the back of the church to start walking down the aisle, I felt pale and gothic, my jet-black hair pinned back in a chignon. I was the last one to go and I walked too fast so that Kat had to wait an extra long pause until it was her turn to go. During the 'I do's my nose started bleeding and the mother of the groom, who was sitting in the front row, had to scramble around for a tissue and lean over to hand it to me. Kat stood up daintily on the raised platform and grinned back at me as I swept across the front of the church and got the laughs. 'I'm so sorry!' I told her afterwards. 'I didn't meant to take your limelight!' Her hug was warm and loving.

'Lorelei,' she said. 'It wouldn't have been right if you hadn't got a nosebleed.'

At the reception I caught the bouquet. 'I knew it!' Kat cried. 'You're next!' Outside on the street, I waited till last to say goodbye to her and when we hugged I felt her hands slipping against the satin of my dress as I clung to her. Tears overcame me and I wanted to keep holding onto her forever, my oldest friend who loved me for who I used to be, but she moved off into the crowd, bending down low to keep her hairstyle intact as she stepped into the car and waved to us out the window. Her husband started up the engine, and they were gone.

Twenty-five

Once upon a time

Twenty

Twenty-one

Twenty-three

Twenty-four

Twenty-five

Twenty-six

Twenty-seven

Twenty-eight

Thirty

I was in a fog, barely aware of the world outside my head. I started a routine on weekends of reading the newspaper, trying to catch up. Schapelle Corby arrested, George W. Bush inaugurated for a second term as US president, Prince Charles and Camilla getting married, Arthur Miller and Hunter S. Thompson dead.

I felt displaced in Melbourne. I'd moved out of Reuben's place very quickly after everything had fallen apart and found a temporary sharehouse in Fitzroy. Then my friend Gill from Brisbane moved down. We decided to live together. I was working hard to get off the antidepressants and decide what to do next, and she was trying to make a new start in Melbourne too. Gill was bright and funny and into art and music; she carried a sketchbook around everywhere and was always drawing. We moved to Carlton and spent our days hanging out and listening to music, standing in queues to hand in our dole forms or driving to faraway op shops in her car. We saw a sign for a free positive thinking course in Fitzroy and went to one class, but Gill couldn't stop laughing and said it was a cult so we didn't go back. I tried to write short stories and worked slow nights at the cinema. When our friend Hannah moved down, life seemed to start up again.

Hannah smelt like cigarettes and *Une Fleur de Cassie* perfume. She had long black hair with a fringe and she looked like a sixties singer. I had known her since my Brisbane days, and even before she arrived we'd talked about starting our own band together. From the beginning we were borrowing each other's clothes, going out to gigs, having long conversations about books and music and tips on surviving with hardly any money. The three of us decided to look for a house together.

Househunting in Melbourne is the worst early in the year when competition is at its peak due to people starting new jobs and university courses and everyone just generally trying to begin their lives afresh. Each Saturday Hannah, Gill and I would wait out on the grass in front of a terrace house, trying to psyche out the others who were also sitting there competing for the chance to rent it. The moment the real estate agent arrived, we'd jump up and push ourselves past everyone else to check out the rooms, then topple out to the inevitably overgrown backyard and snatch an application form from the agent, determined to be the first to fax it in that afternoon.

The sheet of paper was like a prized skinned scalp as we ran back to talk it over in the car and dash to the next, maybe-it'll-be-better open house.

It was a two-storey Victorian terrace in North Melbourne that we eventually called home. It had ugly lino around the perimeters retreating from decades-old carpet, which spread out from the central living room like dank wet newspaper. We had asked our friends who worked in galleries, or who had proper jobs in film and photography, with job titles and letterheads, to write us references, and then dressed up in smart op-shop blouses and pencil skirts to walk to the real estate office and hand in our applications personally. Under the guise of being young professionals we got the house, and then we started a band called exactly that: Young Professionals. We rehearsed at night in our living room scrawling lyrics on the backs of unpaid electricity bills, and roamed the streets during the day in a pack.

One afternoon when we were out, I saw Reuben walking down the street and the shock hit me hard. But now I had somewhere to put the feeling, of anger, frustration and confusion. With these girls by my side, I didn't have to feel it on my own. We got home and wrote our first proper song with music and called it 'Smug Man'. We used the instruments we already accidentally owned: a bass, a guitar, a Casio Rapman, tambourines and an omnichord, which is like an electronic harp. Hannah had found it in an op shop. Not knowing how to play any of them properly, we swapped around and tried them all. We borrowed a drum kit and played it standing up because it was easier to hit it hard from a height.

By the time my birthday came around we had written five songs and were ready to play our first show in the living room. About twenty of our friends squeezed in to watch us perform, along with another band that had just started, Midnight Juggernauts. We had one tinny mic that we passed around to each other, and everything was drowned out by the tambourine, which one of us was always shaking. We were shambolic, we had no idea what we were doing. The resulting performance was crazy and brilliant.

Our second show was at a big warehouse party where everyone arrived in elaborate costumes and left half-naked and soaking wet from plunging into the onsite hot tubs. People were packed in and stood close enough to touch us as we played. Before long the mix of electricity and water in the room made everything short-circuit. We overheard someone in the audience saying, 'If they get any better, they'll be shit' and we realised it was okay to not know what we were doing. That our strength was in being orchestratedly and amazingly messy.

We had to organise our own gigs at the start: we were outsiders and we didn't know anyone. But the more shows we played, the more friends we made—other people and bands who we kept seeing around at gigs—and soon we were playing regularly.

It was liberating to be so ramshackle, to not know what we were doing. I'd always tried hard to be good at things, but now I was with people who didn't care about that, at least not in a conventional way. People seemed drawn to our out-of-time, shouty music, and although we fumbled around on our instruments, stopping and starting a lot, our name that graced the posters and flyers we painted on Gill's bedroom floor stated the truth: we were a real band. I went from skulking around town, hiding out, not knowing when the ghosts of my former life might show up, to being on stage and not caring.

Gradually we stopped swapping around instruments and I settled on bass, Gill on guitar and Hannah on keyboard. The music was basic post-punk rock'n'roll. Gill was obsessed with upstrokes so our songs always sounded like they were teetering, and we'd alter the rhythm and mood suddenly, unexpectedly, right in the middle of a song. We didn't know how to smoothly change gears, so we just made a point out of it being abrupt. Nearly every gig we had to find a new drummer: no one ever drummed for us for more than a few shows but it didn't matter—our songs were so basic anyone could jump up and fill in. Sometimes one of the boys we were seeing played, sometimes it was just anyone who liked our music and wanted to help out.

We used an ironing board as a keyboard stand and Hannah kept her tobacco and filters and lighter on the edge of her keyboard and smoked through every show. She had written the notes from A to G on each key with a Sharpie pen. I stuck tiny squares of masking tape on my bass guitar with the notes written on in the right position too. Gill never needed to write the notes on her guitar because she already knew them.

I dyed my hair red. We planned our on-stage outfits like we planned the set lists. Everyone in Melbourne seemed to be wearing skinny jeans, but we had a strict No Jeans Allowed rule. Instead we wore floral dresses with sparkly stockings, denim shorts with blouses in block colours and men's ties, lace camisoles with pencil skirts. We recorded an EP in Hannah's bedroom, a microphone dangling down from the light fixture in the centre of the room that we all sang into. We stamped our feet along as we played. No one ever sang one song all by themselves, it was always the three of us.

Hannah and Gill found a stray dog wandering on Brunswick Street and named him What-a-Mess—a scruffy, bitey, dirty-white mutt. He would sit sleepily on the couch and watch us rehearse and play records we'd just discovered to each other. There was The Shags, The Slits, The Raincoats, The Monks. One day, we'd been practising the Iggy and the Stooges song 'I Wanna Be Your Dog'. It was just three chords, the notes repeating over and over, like walking down three steps, logical and beautiful, before starting back at the top note as if the last three steps never happened. We stood in a line across the living room and played, singing the words as a group, in a monotone. Hannah just had to hit one note on her keyboard over and over in quick staccato, like she was typing on a typewriter with one finger. The song was so easy she could even use her other hand to smoke at the same time. I looked over at them—Hannah, whose hair usually cascaded down over her face as she played, Gill's shaggy blonde mane that made her look like Kurt Cobain—and they both looked up at me. Suddenly I realised that I could play and look at the others at the same time too, without messing it up. We started laughing, astonished as we all realised together we were still playing in unison.

'Holy shit,' cried Hannah. 'We're playing a real song.'

'Let's never stop!' said Gill. We kept grinning at each other and cracking up as we played on and on.

Our first show at a proper venue was the night of the federal election in 2004. It was at Ding Dong, with its silver curtains and a toilet queue you could linger in for hours, chatting, your drink shakily balanced on the edge of the sink as you watched girls do their lipstick, or drugs. We were used to coming here to watch our friends' bands but now we were lugging the huge ironing board through the room, headed to an area we'd never been before, the man-packed backstage area.

An AC/DC tribute band was also playing that night and its members were puzzled when we arrived.

'Doing some ironing are we, ladies?'

'It's for our keyboard,' Hannah said, as if it should be obvious.

I was wearing a repurposed red velvet dress, originally made for a little girl. I'd retrieved it from Mum's cupboard on a recent visit home, and despaired that it was too small for me. But Mum had cut it up the centre and transformed it into a cape so I could still wear it. It felt magical on, stiff and structured at the shoulders, with a quilted bodice, and then flowing out into a regal wave, strips of gold bordering its velvet kingdom like palace walls. I'd never worn it as a kid—the fabric seemed too rich and opulent to play in and so it had just sat in the wardrobe. Now, fully grown, I revelled in it being the most perfect dress to play in. Underneath it I wore a black leotard and stockings.

On stage, we flanked each other like security guards, standing in a straight line across the front of the stage. We played the songs we had written in our living room, about men, about not being in love with them, about their pretentious record collections, about throwing up on them by accident. When we finished we collapsed backstage, excited, exhausted. The sweat had stained black the underarms of my red cape but I didn't care. The marks were like emblems, badges to be proud of. The AC/DC tribute band started playing around the same time the news reached us that John Howard's conservative government had got back in. We got drunk. Later at home the three of us danced, smoked, made up more songs and drew tattoos on each other. I stripped off the cape, and Hannah said, 'You know, we should all just always wear leotards at the shows. Or swimsuits. Like a uniform.' And from then on, we did. Dressing in a swimsuit and stockings was easy to do when there were three of us. It didn't feel weird like it might have if I was up there on my own.

We got a manager and she started getting us better gigs. One night we opened for The Dirty Three. When we got out on stage, we saw the audience was mostly made up of guys, their arms folded, assessing us suspiciously. But right up front we had our usual gang of girls who came to every show: seven or eight women from the shop where Hannah worked, dancing with arms whipping, hips side-to-side swinging, back and forward. We stood up there like seahorses, bending our necks downwards to check what our fingers were doing, and up again briefly to see the girls in the front with their cigarettes jumping up and down in a mad frenzy. At the end we decided to do an encore, which was not expected because we were the first band on, but we didn't care. We threw down our instruments and smashed our drum kit and shook each other by the shoulders, pelting our tambourines and maracas onto the floor, and then we left the stage to go and drink with our friends. We were having such a good time with each other we forgot to come back in and watch the headline band.

But as we settled into Melbourne, our lives got busier. Hannah was writing for *Vice*, Gill had started jamming with other bands, and I'd gone back to uni to study editing and publishing. As I became more settled in Melbourne I felt like I was battling two parts of myself: one that wanted to perform and play music and one that was pulled towards writing and discussing books with nerdy literary friends. Rehearsals were getting more difficult to organise as our time and priorities were splintered in different directions. And there were times when it didn't feel like the three of us anymore; it felt like Gill and Hannah, who had moved to a new place together, and then me.

By the time we played Meredith, a music festival outside of Melbourne, in December 2005, we could afford a real keyboard stand. It was supposed to be a two-hour drive, but

four hours later we were still sitting in traffic a few kilometres
from the entrance to the festival site. We were due on stage in
an hour. Suddenly, Gill swerved and sped along the shoulder
of the road. Idiotically, we waved our band passes out our
windows at everyone. We made it to the stage with twenty
minutes to spare, changing in a caravan into our uniform of
swimsuits and stockings and heels. I teased my hair, pinning
it up high into a bird's nest; Hannah's fell loose and straight as
always. She clenched her teeth in a big, mock-confident smile.
Gill swigged at a cold beer, grinning, going around to all of
us and patting our shoulders reassuringly. It was time. On
heeled hooves we pranced across the dirt towards the stage.
Peeking out from the wings, I felt Hannah's fingers squeeze
my arm. The crowds at Meredith reached up to 13,000, and
although it was early the crowd was already in the thousands.
People stuck out of the hills like birthday candles, most of
them there to stake out prime positions where they could
watch the popular acts later on. They weren't there to see us.
The sun was still up because of daylight saving. It felt like we
were about to play during lunchtime at school.

We walked on to a patter of applause and saw a few of our
friends right up the front holding their cans of beer. The stage
was huge and I felt far away from Hannah and Gill, like we
were floating on ice caps. We started playing but couldn't hear
ourselves in the foldback, so we compensated by screaming

louder than usual. We knew we probably sounded terrible, but we couldn't get across the stage to each other to talk about it and fix it. I felt chained to my bass amp like a dog on a leash. When I looked up, I could see people in the crowd talking to each other, distracted, not watching.

The sun had almost set when we finished. We were released out into the night, into the festival, relieved it was over. The temperature had dropped quickly like it does in the hills. We usually walked back out together after a gig, all of us, to get a drink, but I was cold so I went back to the tent to change. 'Come back, we'll be here,' they said.

When I returned, another band was playing and I couldn't find Hannah or Gill. I got a drink, watched the band, wandered. I took a pill and went on the ferris wheel with strangers. I tried to enjoy being lost in the dark, in the crowd, imagining I could be anyone, but wishing I would see someone I knew soon.

'Hey, you're from that band.' A stranger grabbed me and stopped me. Being recognised was like being embraced. I waited for them to talk to me more, but they kept walking and I felt myself disappear into the dark again. As I wandered, everyone looked the same: everyone looked like Hannah, tall with long black hair and a fringe. Everyone looked like Gill, shaggy hair and jeans and a swagger. I felt a shivery loneliness as the sun came up.

We were supposed to stay the whole weekend but I caught a lift back to Melbourne that morning without the others. When I got home I took a hot shower and curled up into bed under the doona by myself, trying to get warm again.

I didn't see Hannah or Gill after Meredith until Christmas and New Year had come and gone and we reconvened for band practice at Gill and Hannah's sharehouse in North Carlton. I'd also just moved and now lived on the same street. I walked the two blocks to their house with my bass slung across my body. It was sweltering hot, the day of the Big Day Out, which that year was happening close by in a park in Carlton. We sat around smoking, wishing we had enough money to go and see Iggy and the Stooges, who were playing. We didn't talk about Meredith, how we'd been so distant on the stage and then how I'd lost them afterwards. I couldn't shake the loneliness, the separateness I'd felt. No one could say it just yet, but we were heading in different directions. We didn't need to cling to each other as much anymore. The danger of being alone in a new and big city had passed and now it was safe to go off on our own.

Hannah and Gill went out to buy cigarettes. I decided to stay and wait for them, but Gill ran back inside to get me. 'You have to come out here!' She had a huge smile on her face.

'Lorelei, get out here!' I heard Hannah yelling from the street. As I ran outside I could hear the sound faintly, and all of a sudden as I reached the corner it rang out clearly, carried on the heat, cutting across to us over the blue January sky. In amid the rosemary bushes and magnolias, we were hit with the bassline cascading across Princes Park all the way to us, those three notes, like walking three steps over and over, one keyboard note, pointing, pounding. We stamped our feet, jumping up and down on the concrete footpath, screaming happily and as loud as we could. 'Now I wanna! Be your dog!' We clasped each other's wrists, shaking our heads of hair, and I wished we could keep playing like this forever.

Twenty-six

The job interview was at an office out in the suburbs, almost an hour from the city, on a road lined with industrial complexes like a never-ending sentence. I'd decided I wanted to get a proper job. I wanted to become a professional and everything that implied: the outfits, the salary, the attitude. Become someone who knew what she was doing, who had direction, who could make decisions. When I enrolled in a postgraduate editing and publishing degree I had to go for an interview at the university and the course director told me straight out: 'We don't accept anyone who isn't already working in the industry.' I stared down at the hem of my dress. I wasn't leaving. 'But I *have* to do this course,' I pleaded. 'I've got nothing else.' He must have sensed my desperation because he let me in.

Now, six months into my studies, I finally had an interview for an editorial assistant job. I wore the bottle green wool dress my mum had made for herself to wear at my brother's christening twenty years earlier. A moth had eaten a small, delicate triangular hole at the front, so I wore it backwards. With an enormous dictionary in front of me, I slowly worked through the proofreading test the way I'd been taught, line by line, checking every spelling with the dictionary, examining every punctuation mark twice. I used the full hour they'd given me and when they phoned the next day to say I had got the job, I didn't even hear what the salary was, or if I did hear it the numbers didn't mean anything to me. I was only interested in words.

From that first day in the office, editing felt right. The work straightened my back; I sat purposefully at a desk like I belonged there. Being an editor meant learning how to find out what was wrong and fix it. There, on the page, things could almost be perfect. This was where I could create order. Everything looked so clear when you were looking down at a piece of paper, as if you were seeing it through binoculars. Editing asked the questions I had been wondering myself about everything: *What does this mean?* Of every word and every sentence, you have to ask: *What is the point of this?* Being an editor also meant being invisible—you did work no one noticed unless it was bad. As a third daughter who had always felt starved for attention, I was surprised to find I didn't mind that.

It took three hours to get to work by public transport, so I got up at 5 a.m. when it was still dark. I'd catch the tram to the city, hop on a train to the last stop and from there, a bus would take me the few extra kilometres to the office in the south-eastern suburbs. On the way I studied my editing textbooks, absorbed in this new world of rules and structure, of deadlines and schedules.

After a few months of this, another editor who lived near me, Niki, offered to drive me. It cut the journey down to an hour, and on the way she regaled me with all the gossip— stories from before I had arrived at the company. One day we pulled up to the lights at the train crossing at Springvale Road. The crossing was notorious; people were sometimes killed there because they'd been trapped in their cars when the boom gates came down. We were sitting behind a line of cars waiting for them to open when Niki asked me why, seeing as I had done an undergrad in writing, I wanted to be an editor and not a writer. 'I mean, you do your own writing on the side, too, right?'

'Not anymore,' I told her confidently. 'I just want to publish my friends.' I'd been thinking of all the talented young writers I'd met through my undergraduate degree in Brisbane and later on in Melbourne. This, to me, seemed like a great ambition, to get their work out there. I didn't think of myself as being a writer anymore. It didn't seem professional, it didn't have a clear enough path, one I could point to and say, 'This is what I do.' I had felt lost for so long; now I craved a road to follow.

I loved dressing for my job. Every morning I took time to get ready in front of the mirror. I started to notice specific things about myself that could be improved, like my thighs and my arms. For the first time, women's magazines seemed relevant to me. I devoured the articles and felt like they were speaking to me. 'Six easy work outfits!', 'The busy woman's guide to shoes.' I worked hard, so now I deserved things. I started spending the small amount of money I had left over after rent on a modest wardrobe reformation. I'd never bought brand new clothes before. I chose practical pieces: a sleek cardigan, singlet tops, a classic black dress and pointy shoes with a small heel. And every month, I looked down at my pay slip, a piece of paper, and smiled. The numbers were splintered like woodchips into separate pieces that didn't concern me: superannuation, debt I'd accrued through my tertiary fees, tax, the social fund, and at the very bottom was a number left over and that was mine. It was more than I'd ever had and it felt like a miracle.

I moved to a new apartment in the inner city with Emily, another professional woman who was so organised and grown-up she owned framed posters and new furniture. We had two floors with two bathrooms and an enormous living space. It was decadent and adult—I felt like I'd finally got somewhere. Emily and I had dinner parties, but it wasn't like my terrible attempts back when I lived with Jack. Emily knew how to cook, and introduced me to food I'd never bothered trying before like edamame and ruby red grapefruit, and also to her friends—other young women who had jobs and professional ambitions too. We wore patterned summer dresses and had people over and drank wine and gossiped about our bosses and our working hours and our career goals.

One day, Jack arrived in town. He'd recently broken up with a girl in Brisbane and I said I'd leave a key out for him, so he could sleep on our couch until he found somewhere else to live. He packed all his records and belongings into a truck and drove down. When I got home from work he was there. I kicked off my pointy shoes and hugged him.

He stepped back and looked at me. 'You've changed,' he said.

'I know!' I said happily. 'But it's not bad, is it?'

'No, it's just new.'

I'd spent the days before Jack arrived wondering in the back of my mind whether I'd still like him, maybe even love him, but during the week he stayed I saw how all he now cared about was seeing bands and partying. I still liked him but felt way beyond that now, like I'd shrugged off a dress I was attached to but that had got too small for me a long time ago and I'd only just noticed. There was no time for such things anymore—and yet it was comforting to see Jack again, to have someone who knew who I was underneath all these newer layers of Melbourne. I liked him being there, knowing he was asleep downstairs with his cheek resting heavily on the pillow of his palm, but after a few days he left, found a sharehouse, and drifted away into his own life.

One day on the way to work, Niki asked: 'Why don't you get a car?'

I was shocked. 'Um, because I could never afford one.'

'Yes, you could. You could get a car loan.'

I had never heard of such a thing. At Niki's advice, I went to the car dealership the next Saturday morning and, bewitched by the shine of the car metal and cheesy smiles of the dealers, I took one for a test drive. When I got back all the paperwork had already been done. All I needed was to prove to them I earned a salary so I could afford the repayments every week, and I suddenly had a brand new car. It was like a magic trick.

Every morning I hit the road by 8 a.m. and drove away from the city into the suburbs, and gradually I moved up from editorial assistant to trainee editor, and at last to editor. I started commissioning authors and illustrators, becoming more confident at being able to see a manuscript from a single idea to a printed, bound book. I started to see where this career could go—to publishing fairs in Italy and Germany if I worked hard enough, and maybe even to the mecca of publishing: New York. At last I was moving forward.

I was losing touch with my old friends. I kept trying to catch up with Jack, but he was always busy. Sometimes I went to gigs on weekends but it was hard to keep up. I went to all the familiar places but I couldn't enjoy myself; all I could think about was how I had to get up early the next morning for work. Hannah and Gill started a new band and I went to see them play but it made me feel terrible to not be a part of it. I left straight afterwards, feeling old. Girls I'd met in toilet lines and had briefly become best friends with, boys in bands I had played shows with, would smile and say hello as if they knew me but now I struggled to place them. I dug feebly around for their names, trying to excavate a memory, a recollection of rolling around pashing with them on the floor or a night spent wandering through a park together talking in weird accents—but it all seemed so long ago.

I'd known a guy called Nathan when I was in the band, a sound engineer, and we started hanging out more. We cooked and talked, and on weekends drove my car out of the city, to bed-and-breakfasts in the country and on daytrips to the beach. After a few weeks, I realised I'd accidentally got a boyfriend, a really nice one, a quiet one, who introduced me to his family and friends and made me feel a part of things again. Small and pleasant things: a TV series, a new band or restaurant. It felt good to be with him.

When I'd first met Jack, I wanted to let him in on every-thing, tell him all about my past. With Reuben, I had been impressed by him and wanted to impress him—I was swept up completely. Now, with Nathan, I felt like it was a fresh start. I wanted him to think I was together, that I knew what I was doing. It was the first relationship I'd had that matched the job and the apartment in terms of maturity. With surprise, it dawned on me that I now had the trifecta. I had always wondered how people became themselves, how they grew up. It seemed so organised, planned when you looked at it from the outside, as if they had known all along what they had to do, but now I was in on the secret too.

If you got a proper job, you could get a car. Once you had a job and a car, your back started hurting from sitting and driving all the time, so that's when you started doing yoga. But because you got up early to do yoga, you had to go to bed early. So you stopped going to gigs, and did the grocery shop-ping every Sunday night because you needed to take lunch in to work for the week ahead. Now you even kept the discount fuel offer at the bottom of the docket.

I felt like I had escaped from a world where everything was loud and lost. Nathan was sturdy and he anchored me, but he went overseas for work a lot, calling me from Iceland, from Spain, from London. We emailed and grew closer with the thousands of words exchanged every week, but when he wasn't there I felt shaky, unsure again about what I was doing. One weekend when Nathan was away, I didn't know what to do with myself. I hadn't brought any work home like I usually did. I called Jack to see if he wanted to come with me to the Camberwell market, but he was still in bed, so I went there alone and stumbled across a birdcage pushed to the edges of one of the stalls, bone white and attached to a tall, elegant stand. I bought it, fuming at Jack. Didn't he remember our time together, everything we'd been through? I thought of the canary we had bought together, Gus, who sang beautifully from the moment we brought him home. As much as I yearned to move forward, I kept getting stuck in the old times. It's not that I wanted them back, I just wanted them to have meant something.

At my next stop, the pet shop at the Victoria Market, there were three canaries for sale. I chose the bird that was the butteriest yellow. I called him Zooey and he sat beside me in his perforated shoebox as I drove home very carefully. It took him a week to start singing. The first chirps I heard were little coughs, as though he was sick, but one day when I got home from work he was trilling a snippet of a tune. I sat down and watched him skipping with his little beak wide open and it made me feel so happy.

My job was going well but if I didn't have any work to take home and Nathan was away, I was at a loose end. So like a mature person with a proper job, I thought I should take some extra-curricular classes. I thought about the things I liked to do. I still loved to sing and dance, so I enrolled in a class called Beginners Adult Ballet. I bought pink tights and ballet slippers and a pale purple leotard that felt soft and furry against my skin. To my first class I wore my hair in braids pinned to the top of my head. The teacher made us push our feet out like pointed little broomsticks and scrape them across the floor, in half moons. My feet kept cramping but the wordlessness of movement was a respite. It was calming to stop using words for two hours every week, to feel things in my muscles again, like I had felt years before in love with Jack or Reuben, like I had felt onstage playing in the band. Startled, I wondered if I felt that same intoxicating feeling with Nathan, but with my pointed toes moving in crescents across the floorboards I swept the question quickly from my mind. That intoxicating feeling had never got me anywhere, so why trust it anyway.

Next I found a classical singing teacher so that instead of screeching like Courtney Love I could learn to use my voice properly. My teacher lived in a small ground-floor apartment and I felt sorry for her neighbours. I went in for my first lesson feeling confident: I'd taken lessons as a teenager, belting out show tunes such as 'What I Did For Love' from the musical *A Chorus Line* and I hoped these classes would be like that again, full of songs that were brassy and strong. But at the first lesson the teacher just made me concentrate on my breathing.

For the first three months, in fact, we just breathed. When I was eventually allowed to make a noise, it was one note, a single sound that I had to sustain on one breath.

As the year wore on, I felt more tired, not grown-up and proper like a woman on the make. I missed Nathan, who had now been gone for two months. I started wearing the same things to work day after day. The new clothes I'd bought with my salary were already falling apart; the cardigan became misshapen after one autumn's wear, the synthetic fabrics of the new tops scratched my skin. I reverted to my trusty old dresses.

One night I went to the opera by myself. It was *La bohème* and I bought a box seat. I read the synopsis. Amid a background of crushing poverty two young people fall in love, but then they break up because they just can't make it work. At the end, she dies. A middle-aged couple sat next to me and introduced themselves, Harry and Julie. It was the three of us; a seat remained empty next to me for the date I didn't have. In my long, figure-hugging black dress with gold thread running through it like electricity, I felt overdressed: Harry and Julie were wearing jeans and T-shirts.

The performance started and Harry gave me his binoculars so I could see the performers. I remembered when I was growing up and my mum would play her favourite operas, moving around to them as she did the housework. I used to think the women sounded so old and warbling. But now I heard in the depth of their voices something else—they had experi-enced all there was to experience. It was a marvel to discover that the roles they were playing were actually supposed to be young, beautiful women, who usually die for love. Their voices, far more mature than the ages of the characters they were playing, communicated a youth that was rich and experienced and knowing. Dying for love! It seemed ridiculously, well, operatic. Sitting there, my mind wandered and my thoughts glided across to my own singing and ballet lessons. When you are a kid, these extra-curricular classes lead to something. An end-of-year recital or performance, or at least a certificate. My classes as an adult weren't going anywhere. Soon I would be twenty-seven, then thirty, then fifty. What would I ever do with all my barre stretches and tedious breathing exercises? I decided that when the singing semester ended, when the ballet semester ended, I wouldn't go back.

Nathan came home, and I was thankful and threw myself into his arms. The canary sang in his cage like a flute. Nathan was back for a few weeks, and we spent every summer second we could together. I was in love again. We lay on his lawn in Brunswick under the washing line, hidden by the long grass and the weeds that had grown thick, and we talked. Just two disembodied voices coming out of the grass. I stayed away for nights at a time, phoning my flatmate Emily to ask her to make sure Zooey had fresh water and food in his cage.

Nathan left again, this time for America, and I went back
to waiting. I blew the husks of seed from Zooey's cage and
his puffed-up yellow plumage made me sad. He became
mute. I read that he'd stopped making sounds because he
was moulting, and that he would sing again soon. There were
feathers like strewn petals, along with grit and husk, all over
the tiles. I swept daily but every morning there was more.

Jack lumbered over to visit one night, after weeks of
cancelling on me. He had a new swagger and was confident—
much more than he used to be. It annoyed me. He was starting
to learn how to be a sound engineer too, to make records and
operate the sound desk at music venues. I introduced him to
Zooey. 'Another canary, hey?' he said, but that was all. I'd
always felt that our canary, Gus, had made the apartment
I'd shared with Jack a real home, but after I left for Melbourne
Gus had gone to live with my parents, and a little while later
he'd escaped from his cage and flown into the bush. He would
have died out there.

Jack told me about the jobs he was starting to get, about a
show he'd worked at, and I tried to be excited for him, but all
I felt was left out.

'Nathan sounds nice,' said Jack, out of nowhere, and I
nodded.

'He is. Really nice.'

I'd bought a bottle of red wine and cooked one of my new

recipes that Emily had taught me, a vegetarian lasagne. We chatted, and I told him my car had to go in for a service and I still didn't know how I would afford it.

'I must be so bad with money,' I said, flustered and trying to pour the béchamel from the heavy saucepan into the dish. 'I never have any.'

'No, you've always been good with money,' he said, and I turned to him with surprise. 'You just hardly earn anything at that job.'

'Are you serious? I earn heaps!'

'No, you don't.'

He reminded me I hadn't been able to afford to fly up to Queensland for my dad's sixtieth earlier in the year—I had to ask my parents to help me pay for the airfare. How now I was always talking about how hard it was to pay for petrol, in general conversation. He told me I should stand up for myself and ask for a raise at work. I wiped my hands clean on my apron and grabbed a notebook, jotting tips down as he gave me a pep talk.

Be firm with them, you deserve this, I scribbled. Then, underlined three times at the bottom, the advice Jack had stressed to me was the most important when I was in there asking for a raise: *WHATEVER YOU DO, DON'T CRY.*

When he left I gave him a big hug, genuinely grateful that he'd helped me make a correction when I hadn't noticed the error. I felt certain that if I could just get a bit more money all the restlessness and dissatisfaction would dissolve and I would see again how good my life was.

The night before Nathan came back from America Zooey was more puffed up than usual. He looked so sad and sick. I brought the cage upstairs to my bedroom, and when I woke the next morning he was huddled on the newspaper at the bottom, weak and shivering. I lifted the door of the cage and took him out. He didn't resist or move away like he'd always done before if I tried to pick him up. I held him in my hands and I felt his warm, quivering heartbeat, and as the distance between those gentle thuds became further apart I looked helplessly around me for some way to stop it from happening. My bedroom, with its band posters and books and dresses poking out of the precious, grown-up, built-in wardrobes, held no clue. His whole body trembled and stiffened, and he died in my hands. I didn't know what else to do, so I put the stiff body with a dead heart in it back into the cage and waited. When Nathan arrived a few hours later, all my excitement at seeing him had vanished. My grown-up apartment had every mod con in it, but it didn't have a garden, so we drove to Nathan's house and buried Zooey in his backyard.

I delayed asking for the promotion, dithered for weeks. I was scared. I hated talking about money, and in my field you are supposed to just feel grateful for even having a job. On the day I finally decided to do it, I wore a dress I had bought to wear to the opening night of a film festival back in Brisbane. It had been such a fun night where I'd drunk French champagne and danced and met actors and writers and felt like I was at the centre of art and life. I hadn't put it on since, as if wearing it somewhere else would erase that beautiful memory.

But I was going to make a new one in it today. Moments weren't momentous unless you made them so. The detail of the dress was exquisite—small lace patterning all over the fabric and a big collar that made me think of Lauren Bacall. A pin-tucked heart-shaped bodice that felt like armour against my chest, bolstering me and making me want to pull my shoulders back. My neck became longer and the prickly tickle of the synthetic fifties fabric against my bare legs made me stand tall.

I walked into my boss's office. She was smart and friendly and I had always liked her. When I made my speech, nervously and stammering, I knew she was listening. Nodding. Understanding. I was getting my point across. Clearly and professionally. I hit my stride. I told her I'd been there a long time, and listed all the things I was now responsible for. Then I asked for a small raise that would amount to fifty dollars extra a fortnight. 'I wouldn't ask, but I can barely afford to pay for petrol,' I said, trying to make it seem funny and absurd, with a little laugh that turned, beyond my control, into tears. They rolled down my face, onto the tiered, tired bodice of my dress. They stopped there, caught like a trap by the love-hearted pleats.

My boss handed me the box of tissues on her desk. She smiled kindly and said, 'I'm sorry, but you have to understand our position. We simply can't afford to give you a raise.' She went on to say how much I was appreciated, but that what they were paying me was the standard salary that all editors of my skill and experience were paid and she simply couldn't budge on it.

I walked out feeling so young, like a girl, like all those operatic women who stupidly die for what they love. It seemed so pathetic. My car was being serviced and I was relieved to get out of the office to go and pick it up. The mechanic handed me the bill, which was almost three hundred dollars. 'You're going too tough on the brakes, darl,' he said. I silently handed him my credit card and drove back into the work carpark. I stared at all the cars laid out. The boss's own car was a luxury one. So was, now I thought about it, the guy from accounts, and the people who worked in marketing and sales. I parked next to Niki's car, which looked like an older and rustier version of my own. This is what it will always be like, I despaired.

I was on a publication deadline and had to keep working as my colleagues left for the day. When I finally got on the road, it was raining. I switched on the windscreen wipers and they scraped scratchily over the glass. The mechanic had taken out the old ones but had forgot to replace them. I kept having to reach out and wipe the windscreen with my hand.

I couldn't see a thing. The road was shining and wet, the rain deafening. I tried to keep track of the lane markings, the ellipsis of white paint dot-dot-dotting forever into the distance, but I kept losing sight of them and veering shakily out of my lane. When I got to Springvale Road I thought I could make it across the train tracks, but had to brake as the gates suddenly started singing, lights flashing, the boom gates closing. A long line of cars piled up behind me and as I swivelled to look back at them, I realised I was sitting inside the boom gates, not outside them. I started to panic, quickly inching the car back and forth until I was parallel to the tracks, huddled next to the gate in the tiny patch of space as far from the train tracks as possible. I hunched forward trying to make myself small as I heard the train coming. *DON'T CRY*, I repeated, but here I was, crying.

I was getting beeped at again and opened my eyes to see the train had passed and the gates were up. That's when I knew I had to get moving, get out of there.

Twenty-seven

New York felt like home from the moment I walked out of JFK into the smoky night. On the crowded bus to Grand Central I told the guy sitting next to me what I was doing. 'I've come to get a job in publishing and live in New York and stay *forever!*' I knew I sounded like a cliché but I didn't care. I wanted to be one of the famous, glamorous New York book editors, a Jackie, a Judith, a Jonathan. I didn't think I'd ever come back. Who knows what will happen in New York, I said to myself. I might get a job, or get married, or die!

I'd stayed at my job in Melbourne for six more months, just as long as it took to save enough for the flight to New York and three months' rent. Knowing I was leaving made me determined to live more frugally than ever, and I took on extra freelancing jobs in my spare time. Just before I left I'd had a garage sale at my place, where I sold everything I owned—almost everything. I couldn't let go of the dresses

I loved, so I packed them up for storage, and everything else—books, records, furniture—I sold for two dollars each.

I only knew one person in New York: Krystyna, a friend from university, and I was going to stay at her apartment until I found my own place. She met me at Grand Central with a spare pillow in a Target shopping bag that she'd just bought for me, and an awe-inspiring bleached-blonde angular haircut. We piled onto a crowded train. It was April and the night was warm. *Time Out New York*'s cover story was titled 'The Death of the Hipster' and when we got off at Williamsburg and walked down Bedford Avenue, we passed hipsters wielding sleeve tattoos and pork-pie hats, seeming very much alive. I left my suitcase at Krystyna's and she took me to a sidewalk eatery. I drank a Pabst Blue Ribbon, ate a taco and grinned like an idiot as the television accents washed around me.

I slept in Krystyna's bed with her in her tiny room in the apartment she shared with three Americans. The place was so small that the kitchen was just a bench in the living room. Krystyna had lived there for a year already, and was working as an assistant for an industrial designer. She introduced me to bagels with tomato and cream cheese and capers, took me to Union Square to buy a phone and showed me how to look for apartments on Craigslist. I found a sublet in Midtown on the same street as the theatre bookshop, and by my second week in New York I was pointing out directions to other tourists.

Everything fit right, felt right, the same way it had when I'd first moved to Brisbane, to Melbourne, before everything had gone wrong. I knew this time would be different, though. In the mornings the smell of hot dogs and pretzels cooking out on the kerb wafted up to my fifth-floor walk-up. My bedroom looked out onto the street; the bed was set up high like a bunk bed, but underneath, instead of another bed, was a desk I could work from. There, I emailed job applications in the mornings and in the afternoons I went for interviews. I met with anyone who would talk to me, friends of friends of friends; even the most distant connection was a perfectly justifiable reason to email someone and arrange to meet them just for a chat. Anyone could hold the key to a job in publishing, I kept telling myself.

One of the friends of a friend was Zac. We met up for dinner in the East Village a couple of weeks after I arrived. He took me to a restaurant where the bright lighting illuminated his frizzy hair and his dazzling smile after every sentence. We ordered from the macrobiotic menu and nibbled on seaweed. I was charmed. Like everyone else here, he was so hospitable, so nice. When we said goodbye his hug was lingering. A few days later, when the guy I was subletting my apartment from came back and pitched a tent in the kitchen and started sleeping there, I moved over to Zac's couch in Brooklyn. One night later, to his bed.

It was summer in New York. The nights were so sweltering you had to really want someone to agree to sleep with their skin against yours. I really wanted Zac. When I found another apartment on Craigslist to move over to, he borrowed a car to help me. He dragged my suitcase into the foyer of my new place in Brooklyn, a cosy ground-floor apartment near Prospect Park that I would be sharing with one other girl. As a thankyou gift I gave him a copy of *Franny and Zooey*, not the one that I still carried everywhere in my handbag but a new copy I'd bought for six dollars at The Strand. 'You *have* to read it,' I told him, gazing into his eyes. He promised he would. 'I love Salinger,' he said, juggling the book from hand to hand like a football. We kissed in the doorway. 'I'll talk to you soon,' he said and disappeared.

A few days later, Nathan came to New York for work. We'd broken up before I left because I wanted to feel free embarking on this new adventure, but we were still close. In the month since I'd said goodbye to him in Australia so much had already happened. He felt like an old friend from a long time ago and I was looking forward to seeing him. We met at a restaurant and he pulled out a present for me: a bottle of perfume. With a sinking feeling in my stomach, I knew I had to tell him about Zac and when I did he went very quiet. Our food arrived but he didn't touch his plate. I noticed there were tears in his eyes and I felt horrible. I had known it wouldn't be the greatest news, but I hadn't intended to hurt him. I paid the bill and we walked in silence halfway up the street together before he said he wanted to go on alone. I watched him cross the street and disappear.

Living in New York was like living in a story that I told myself.

There was constant chattering, conversing, narrating in my head. I felt as if I was a character in a movie, one I knew the arc of well. You come to New York to make it and not everyone does, but for some reason you're one of the ones who will. I stood outside the apartment where Dorothy Parker had lived, went to the East Village where Madonna had hung out, to St Patrick's Cathedral where F. Scott and Zelda Fitzgerald were married. All the places people had lived and been and stepped made my own story feel bigger because it seemed somehow connected to all these other great ones.

The American publishing scene was so different from the Australian one. New York editors had starry careers; to me, they seemed like rockstars. One morning I had a meeting with a publisher and that same night I saw him being hilarious and witty on a TV talk show. Their work might have been invisible, like all editors' work was, but they weren't. They were celebrities and personalities in their own right, and I wanted to be like them.

I waited in office foyers to be called in to interviews, girls my age in clacky shoes checking me out as they walked through, arms laden with proofs and enormous takeaway coffees, pencils sticking out of their neatly distressed buns. Sometimes they smiled at me. I hadn't brought many clothes with me, so to every interview I wore the same black dress that I had bought at H&M. I was hoping to obtain the E-3 visa, which depended on you bringing skills to an organisation that an American didn't have. The more interviews I had, the more I understood that it was my differences that would make me a success here. I recreated myself as 'the Australian Girl Who Moved to New York' and I loved playing that part. I had never embraced my Australianness in such a way before. I started to speak more clearly. When I heard my voice it sounded bell-like amid the wash of American accents. I listened to it through others' ears and for the first time it sounded exotic.

At last I got a callback at a major publishing house. A smiley, smartly dressed editor walked me around the floor, introducing me to my soon-to-be-colleagues in the children's book department. Through the office windows I caught a glimpse of New York outside—the buildings were swaying and I felt giddy, my grin stretching so wide it was starting to hurt.

I was taken to the Human Resources department where the HR director placed form after form in front of me, explaining my insurance benefits, leave policies and employee entitlements. 'And every year you and your family will get free passes to the Rockefeller Center ice skating rink!' she said chirpily.

This is it, I thought, my heart tightening in hope and disbelief. It's actually happening.

The smiley editor saw me out. 'Now, just to let you know, I still need to go through the paperwork with my bosses,' she said. 'But as far as I'm concerned you've got the job.'

I went home and waited to hear back. After a week of silence, I finally rang her. Someone in HR eventually answered my call and explained they were sorry but they just couldn't hire an Australian: it was too complicated, the paperwork too dense. I was shattered. I scrolled through my phone and called Zac, but he didn't answer. I hadn't heard from him since he'd dropped me off at my new place. At first, I'd thought he was just letting me settle in, giving me breathing space. He's busy with work, I reminded myself, but now, weeks later and still no word from him, I realised what had happened.

There'll be more, I reassured myself. I'm in New York. There's got to be more. Jobs, men, everything. But I was discovering that there were two sorts of days in New York. The days when everything seemed possible, where people would stop on the street and tell me that I had a lovely smile, or I'd be given free tickets to a show, or someone would invite me to their place for dinner. The other sort of day was when I got shoved on the street, or a cab driver was rude and impatient, or when I didn't have enough money even for a bagel and it seemed such a struggle just to climb up the stairs from the subway platform to the street.

By the end of August, the summer was still hanging heavy and four more publishing houses had got so close to hiring me that I thought I had the job, but each time was the same as the first. I'd have a sparkling interview, a callback where I'd be introduced to everyone, and at the last minute be let down because of the paperwork.

I got a job as a dogwalker. Every morning I'd put on jogging shoes and pocket the gigantic bunch of keys my boss gave me. Keys that unlocked various apartments of Brooklyn, each with a trick you had to learn: you had to wriggle it, turn it sharply to the left exactly three-quarters of the way, and push on the door. I had all the secret systems in my notebook, along with all the names of the pets in each apartment: Mister, Lucy, Milo, Buster, Gregory, Jess. One of my jobs took me past Zac's apartment every day, and I gazed up to his bedroom window as I passed but I could never see anything. He'd vanished.

One day, struggling with Billy, an enormous Rhodesian Ridgeback puppy, I noticed some books sitting out on a stoop.

As I approached I saw they were the complete diaries of Anaïs Nin. I quickly counted them: there were six instead of seven—volume four was missing. They seemed to be for the taking so I threw them into my tote bag with the keys, a bottle of water and poop bags. Billy pulled me away. From then on, I read the diaries day and night. I was obsessed. The book mentioned the address of Anaïs's childhood home, on the Upper West Side, and I took the subway and stood outside her old house trying to imagine her there as a young woman. There was no plaque to say she'd been there. As I headed back to the subway, Nathan phoned me from somewhere in the United Kingdom. He was on tour. I was so happy to hear from him. He told me he missed me but I didn't know what to say to that. The line was bad and we had to hang up. I felt sheepish and confused. Waiting on the platform at peak hour with hundreds of people pushing around me, I wondered if I had thrown something away, a life I could have had. More than ever, I had to make this New York thing work or everything would have all been a waste.

I was still broke. Dogwalking wasn't enough. I started working ten-hour shifts at a popular restaurant with a celebrity clientele, and lived off the tips. The city instantly turned around for me. I was once again the Australian Girl Who Moved to New York. I skipped around the restaurant happily, my shiny red ponytail swishing as I bussed food out to customers. I worked six days a week and continued going for publishing interviews on my day off. It was hard, but it made life easy again. One night I met a guy called Joe at an experimental music gig I wandered into, and I went home with him. He was a musician and only lived a few blocks from me. We started hanging out and he rolled joints as we talked about music and art, psychology and Buddhism.

'You use your mind too much,' he said. 'You have to chill out more, be more present.' I started trying to explain there were good reasons for me to be stressed out, that I needed to get a publishing job, that it was all over if I didn't, but he put his hand on my thigh and told me again, 'You just have to chill out.'

The customers at the restaurant where I worked were a combination of celebrities and tourists who hoped to catch a glimpse of a celebrity. There was a door list and a door bitch to enforce it, and regulars who always ordered the same thing. Movie stars and models, screenwriters and photographers had their meetings there, scripts were pored over and deals were done. I was starting to think that my big break could happen here, in this restaurant, not at an interview in an office. Once again, it seemed like anything could happen.

I had to train myself not to gush when sending orders to the kitchen: Maggie Gyllenhaal's smoked chicken sandwich, Terry Richardson's salmon pot pie. It was tempting to make snap judgements about well-known celebrities according to how they treated me as a waitress. I felt almost disappointed to discover that most famous people are generally just polite or taciturn, except for Josh Hartnett who is polite and taciturn and a bad tipper.

It became usual to hand Heath Ledger his coffee. He was well-mannered and quiet and always ordered it to go.

One Sunday morning Elijah Wood came in with his girl-friend. They sat by the window doing the *New York Times* crossword. When I asked them if they'd like another coffee, he looked up at me with startling blue eyes and said he loved my accent. 'Are you from New Zealand?' he asked.

'No, Australia!' I said brightly. 'But I really wish I could live in New York *forever*!' I could feel my ponytail bouncing jauntily. I told him all my troubles, unable to stop myself. His spoon froze mid-air above his granola as he politely listened to my pitch. 'You see, the E-3 visa is new and very difficult to get because employers don't realise that all it takes is two signatures from them—they don't need to pay a cent—and then I can stay here *forever*!' When I finished, I gulped for air.

'Well, good luck, I'm sure it will all work out,' he said, and went back to his granola and crossword.

After work one night I went to a bar and spotted Zac there with a group of people. I marched up to him. I still didn't understand why no one in New York ever phoned you back. 'Why didn't you call?' I asked. 'I really thought we had a connection, you know.'

He looked around uncomfortably. 'Yeah, we definitely had a moment,' he said. He turned back to the bar, so I put my hand on his arm. 'Hey.'

He swung around, irritated. 'Yeah?'

'Did you ever end up reading *Franny and Zooey*?'

'What?' he said.

I pulled my hand away from him and walked out.

On a quiet weekday afternoon, while people ate their late lunches and early dinners, I served a girl sitting by the window. She had flowers pinned in her hair with two braids running around her head like a halo, the same way I often did mine.

'She's Australian too, she's going for a job here,' the manager told me. I decided to take it upon myself to give her some tips for getting the job, and went over and started talking to her.

She got hired, but she never ended up working a day in the restaurant because the very next week a huge story broke across the city. A young guy, a graphic designer, had seen a girl on the subway and fallen in love with her. He made a website called 'NYC Girl of My Dreams' in a bid to find her and posted a drawing he'd done of her, complete with her distinctive braids and flowers. The media loved it. Within forty-eight hours of the website going up she'd been found. I watched her on *Good Morning America* and everyone at the restaurant was talking about it the next day. I seethed at the unfairness of it. I was meant to be the Australian Girl Who Moved to New York!

That night I could barely drag my body up the stairs to my room. I was exhausted. I opened up my computer to check my email, and there was one from an old friend, sitting there like buried treasure amid all the unreplied emails from my family and friends. She had organised an interview for me with a writer. He needed a research and administration assistant. This was it: my final chance to stay in New York.

The dress was blue and it had a stunning feature at the collar—a big bow of transparent lace that made me think of a butterfly. The fabric of the skirt overlapped to hide peekaboo embroidered white flowers that were revealed when you walked. I felt botanical in it. I'd bought it at a second-hand store in Soho a couple of months earlier, unable to resist it after I'd taken it off the rack and held it in my arms. I'm always astonished at how dresses can survive so many years. But they do; while the bodies inside them age, they stay young and shapely and full of hope. The dress made me think of wise-cracking forties secretaries, of the smart glamour of Norma Shearer and the other actresses in *The Women,* my favourite film. In it I felt neat and capable. The night before the interview I hung it up beside my work uniform for the next day and crashed into bed.

All day I didn't have to put on an act of smiling. My tips added up to more than I had ever earnt. In the cramped change room I wriggled out of my uniform, going through what to say at the interview. I carefully drew the dress over my head and held up my arms to poke them into the sleeves. I pushed my head through and carefully tugged at the fabric to get it down over my bust. The skirt fluttered to sit just above my knees. It felt wonderful. I turned to face the mirror and pinched together the two edges of the zip that ran down the side of the dress and cautiously tugged on it. Nothing. Changing positions and using the other hand, I pulled the dress in tighter with my free hand and held my breath, but the zipper wouldn't budge. If I tugged any harder, it would snap. Defeated, I flopped down on the bench seat.

The dress, originally made for an undernourished war bride, had fit me in the change room of the shop months earlier, but it didn't anymore. I tried to compose myself, dug out the jeans and jacket I had worn to work that morning and pinned my hair up into plaits on top of my head. I put on lipstick and plodded to the West Village café where I'd arranged to meet the writer, and waited. Until now I'd always felt there was a possibility of being the next big thing, and now, the dream, the cliché of making it in New York, finally felt very close to being over. I ordered a tea and sat at the window. I took out my notebook and opened it to where I had written a quote from Anaïs Nin: 'Life shrinks or expands in proportion to one's courage.' I took a deep breath.

If we click, we do, I reasoned, and if we don't, we don't. Then I saw him, Malcolm Gladwell, recognisable from his profiles in *The New Yorker* and the back covers of his books *The Tipping Point* and *Blink*, his navy windcheater zipped up against the cold. Gladwell had done lots of research on first impressions. If anyone could tell how desperate I was, he could. Knowing that made me more nervous. I started to fidget. I flashed him an enormous smile when he walked in so he would know it was me. He shook my hand and sat down next to me. I sipped at my tea; he didn't order anything. He explained he was looking for an assistant to help him with research, to keep his appointment book, that sort of thing.

I nodded eagerly, saying 'Absolutely!' to everything.

He asked me what my favourite book was; I said *Franny and Zooey*. He nodded, polite and taciturn like every well-known person I'd come across here. There was a silence. I worried that it was the wrong book, that I was the wrong girl. Feeling my plaits pinned tightly to my scalp and pulling

my hair back painfully, I felt like everything about me
was wrong.

My phone was sitting on the table and I felt it vibrate.
I glanced down. It was a UK number, Nathan calling again.
I turned it round so I couldn't see the screen and, trying
to harness a new, vibrant energy, started reciting the same
story I was always telling strangers in New York. I felt the
words lunge out of me like some unstoppable purge: 'You see,
Malcolm, there's the new E-3 visa and employers don't know
about it so it's been really hard to get a job.' I rambled on and
he sat kindly listening until I was finished. He thanked me
for my time and said he'd call me. I stayed back to pay, to let
him escape, so he wouldn't be embarrassed in case we had to
walk in the same direction. I knew he wouldn't call.

That night riding home on the subway, with the dress
I loved crushed to fit inside my handbag, I noticed the jacket
I was wearing was torn at the sleeves. Everything seemed to
be breaking. I swayed, gripping two paper cups of Sancerre I'd
asked them to pour me at work. I managed large gulps between
stops but it was hard to balance. I lifted my arms to grab on to
the straps and saw my reflection in the dark windows. My tears
showed. I knew I couldn't hold on for much longer.

The next day I went to work at the restaurant for the
last time. I walked past an apartment where a crowd
bubonic with cameras had gathered to watch them bring

out the dead. The collective contagious grief at the sight of a body under a black sheet, the rolling of wheels. I asked someone who it was and they murmured the name of my most polite customer, Heath Ledger. I felt infected by the same weirdly personal–impersonal sadness that now seemed to plague the entire neighbourhood. New York had turned again. It was time to go.

I knew I should call Nathan back, but instead I phoned Joe, who had just been on an ayahuasca trip to welcome in the new year. It was a tribal plant that people used as a hallucinogen.

He told me to come over and as I walked from the train to his house, I was thinking—it was my last resort—I should ask Joe to marry me. But when I arrived there was no time for talking; he pulled me onto the bed straight away. 'Let's try something different today,' he said. He showed me some purple leaves and put them in a clear pipe. 'Salvia,' he told me. 'A hallucinogen from Mexico. Totally legal!'

I sat on the bed and took three hits and when I was conscious again I was lying back on the mattress alone. I didn't know where Joe was. I was floating above everything, on top of the world of the room, and I was laughing. I felt the front of my body zip open and I was in agonising pain, but even though it hurt so much I somehow knew everything was going to be fine. I kept laughing. The pain was so intense that just turning my head to the side seemed like the most difficult thing. I felt like I'd been gone for days but when I saw the clock, I'd only blacked out for four minutes.

Joe came back into the room. 'Sorry, sorry, I had to puke.'

'Joe, I saw yellow giraffes!' I said. 'But they were like people. And there was this little girl in a hat, running back and forth by the window!' I stared into his eyes and he cracked up in delight.

'Will you marry me?' I asked him, suddenly serious.

'What?' he said. My hand clasped his as we lay back and stared at the ceiling. The shapes of the room were reforming themselves back into normal objects: a towel draped over the chair resembled my memory of the giraffes, a wastepaper basket was the girl in the hat.

'Hey, have you read *Franny and Zooey*?' I had forgotten my earlier question, and without waiting for him to answer said, 'Because I have this copy I've been carrying around since I was a kid, since I was fourteen. I would never give it away to anyone because it's so special, but I want *you* to have it.' I punched his chest. 'Because I *love* you.'

'Okay, bring it over some day.'

'I'm leaving tomorrow, Joe! Tomorrow!'

'Well we'd better make the most of it,' he said, and took off his clothes, and then mine.

I wandered back to my house in a daze. It was early morning, and the night waved goodbye, snowing. Everything shone. The garbage trucks had started up, their motors groaning and shifting as they stopped and started. I caught a whiff of the trash each time a bin was picked up, flung upside-down, its contents dropped into the back of the truck. I slept for two hours before the alarm went off and jolted up straight away. I'd planned to take a bunch of clothes to sell, at last, unsentimental and out of necessity because I wouldn't be able to fit them in my suitcase. The big warm jacket I wouldn't need anymore in Australia. The black dress I'd worn to so many interviews. The flat shoes that had pounded the pavement for months. But as I walked, with three garbage bags full, to Beacon's Closet on 5th Avenue, the bags didn't feel so heavy. I stopped at a two-dollar shop and bought a cheap duffel bag instead. I would just take an extra item of luggage back with me, and pay more for it, I decided. At home, as I squashed the clothes into the new bag, I heard a honk downstairs. The cab I'd ordered to take me to the airport was early. I ran down, flustered. 'I'll just be five minutes. Do you mind waiting?' I said to the driver.

'Of course not, miss. Take your time,' she said. Upstairs, packing up my room, I kept looking out the window to check on the cab. The driver was reading a book. I didn't matter to her. I was just another person in this city.

I finally emerged and the driver helped me fit all my bags in the car; they filled up the boot and the whole back seat. I placed the Anaïs Nin diaries out on the stoop. If I'd asked, the driver could have driven past Joe's house, seeing as it was on the way, and I could have left *Franny and Zooey* on his doorstep for him. But instead I put it outside with the other books, for someone else to discover on their own.

Twenty-eight

I sat on my bed back in Buderim, again. Mum and Dad had moved to the top of the mountain when Dad retired, but otherwise everything remained the same. Grandkids, now four of them, tore around the front yard, my parents running after them as tradesmen wandered in and out, working on renovations.

When I had left Melbourne for New York I'd needed to store all my dresses. I'd brought most of them back here in suitcases and garbage bags, shoving them wherever they fit: stuffed into drawers, cupboards and crammed into storage boxes. Now, a year later, I opened the cupboards to be reunited with them and was struck by what I saw. Mum had ironed every dress and stored each one away, packing them neatly in long crates, or hanging them up in colour-coordinated rows. She had transformed my panoply of dresses into a work of art just by arranging them. I skimmed my hand over the fabrics, seeing glimpses of other lives, dresses I had worn and forgotten about: the sapphire-blue fifties satin I'd bought for Jack's birthday one year; the yellow-and-black spotty day dress I'd worn to the park on a summer's day and drunk so much cider I couldn't remember riding home on my bike; the mauve spotted maternity smock I wore with red stockings out on a date with Nathan. They looked so beautiful and impressive the way Mum had arranged them.

But I felt like a failure.

Everything I had planned hadn't happened and now I was back here. But, I assured myself, it wouldn't be for long. I was going to Thailand shortly for my friend Jemima's wedding and when I got back I'd look for somewhere to live in Brisbane.

Jemima and I had known each other since high school. She'd got a job in Thailand at a health resort as a natural therapist a year earlier and met her fiancé there. I had always admired her as someone who knew what she wanted and did it without worrying what other people thought. For me, going to Thailand would be a chance to reset and think about what I wanted to do next, to slow down and maybe have a miraculous life-changing experience too.

I was determined to wear white to the wedding—I had always followed the rule of not wearing white so as not to take attention away from the bride, but because of Thai custom Jemima would be wearing a regal pink gown instead. So I picked out a simple seventies white cotton dress with a small posy of embroidered flowers gathered at the V of the bust line. It was a dress I could imagine myself strolling in, deep in the mountains of Thailand, with a garland of flowers around my neck as small, well-behaved monkeys frolicked at my feet. It would be perfect.

I added it to my pile of dirty clothes, intending to do the laundry later. But while I was out doing last-minute shopping, Mum did it for me. And—either because she had four grandchildren running around her feet, or because she was cooking a special vegetarian feast that night for my farewell, or because, due to the renovations, the washing machine had been disconnected from the water source and had to be filled with a hose pulled in from the backyard—she accidentally threw a red dress into the load of white washing. An hour later every white thing I owned, my undies, singlets and socks, had all turned pink. And the pristine white dress I had planned to wear to the wedding now had a rich, luscious watermelon tint to it—the same colour as Jemima's wedding dress after all.

For half an hour, Mum and I tried to bleach it back to white, squeezing out the dress heavy with water, me trying to hold back tears, the bleach shrinking our hands. Both of us reduced to housewives wringing out laundry.

'Why didn't you just let me do it?!' I snapped.

'I was trying to help!' she threw back.

I stomped back upstairs to find something else I could wear. Mum followed. She was trying to be chirpy and matter-of-fact. 'Well, lucky you've got a thousand other dresses up there you could wear.' I hadn't worn many of them in years and some of them I had never worn—I kept telling myself I was saving them for a special occasion. What special occasion, I had no idea, but I was certain there was nothing as suitable, nothing as light and summery and perfect, for the Thai wedding.

'How about you wear this one?' Mum pulled out a gold and white dress. It had always seemed too glitzy, too gold and girly. Just looking at it on the hanger made me irritated— the fabric had always scratched at my skin and the way the skirt ballooned with air when I walked added an inflated bulk to my lower half. 'I think it'll look great,' she said. 'Try it on.' Her dressmaker's hands felt small and smooth as she did up the zip. 'The empire line suits you,' she added. I could tell she felt bad about the white dress and wanted to help me.

'Well, I hate it,' I replied tetchily. 'It doesn't feel right. It keeps slipping off my shoulders.' As always I struggled to explain exactly why it didn't feel right. 'I feel old in it, middle-aged,' I said finally, and wriggled it off and hung it back up. I felt her annoyance and shrugged. 'What? I just don't feel right in it,' I repeated.

She sighed, and made another pass through the dresses, her fingers flicking through them like they were the pages of a book; they paused momentarily on one and then another before fanning through to the end. Swatches of the dresses she had worn as a young woman flashed by. I wondered how many of her memories were there too.

'You've been wearing the same clothes since you were fifteen. I mean, don't you ever get sick of yourself?' She said distantly. Her voice sounded tense and upset and she went back downstairs without another word.

The gold and white dress had fallen off its hanger like it always did. I was annoyed at Mum for the laundry incident, for making the sort of mistake I would make, the sort that Mums aren't supposed to. But it was true. I *was* sick of myself. Maybe I did need to try something different, something that didn't feel right. I knew Mum wouldn't have lied about it suiting me, so even though I felt uncomfortable in it I decided to trust her. I picked up the dress from the floor and rolled it into a tiny ball. I dug out a pair of heels I'd brought back from New York, and stuffed them both into my backpack. Fine. Done.

When I arrived in the small village south of Bangkok I was reunited with old high school friends and I melted instantly into their embraces. I felt immediately relaxed, being around people who had known me when I was a teenager, back before all the frustrations and false starts of Brisbane and Melbourne and New York. I felt like myself again. The afternoon of the wedding I went to my room to put on the gold and white dress. My skin was already a shade browner from being in the sun. When I turned to look in the mirror the sleeves didn't fall down. The fabric didn't feel scratchy. The dress, for the first time ever, fit.

I drank champagne and threw off my heels and danced on the grass feeling a freedom I hadn't felt in a long time. Giddy, I sat down on one of the plastic chairs on the lawn. My friend Noe, who I had lived with after high school, wandered over and sat down next to me as I rubbed my feet. We looked over at Jemima, newly in love, beaming with happiness. 'She's like a marketing strategy planted in our lives by the department of love and marriage,' I said.

'It's working on me!' said Noe.

'Me too,' I said.

Noe suddenly turned to me. 'What will you do anyway, when you're old, if you don't have any kids to look after you?'

It was a question I'd never thought about, at least not in that way. When I used to think I wanted to have kids, it wasn't so I'd have someone to care for me when I was old. Old age seemed so far away, and my friends were like my family anyway. I expected them to always be around and there for me when I needed them. But as we got older they would all start families of their own. I imagined those of us who would be left—old single women still living in a share-house together, cooking for each other, making cups of tea, watching our favourite TV shows, looking after each other just like we had done throughout our twenties. It actually sounded great. I confidently told Noe about my fantasy. She wasn't so sure. 'Well, yeah, that would be fine for a bit, but what happens when you all start dying? What if you're the last one left?'

Before I could think of an answer, the announcement was made that the bride would be throwing the bouquet. I ran to the front and when Jemima threw the flowers I caught it like I always did. Later, in the early hours of the morning, influenced by champagne, I looked around the wedding party, trying to find someone to kiss. But everyone was too young or too old or too married. With a shock, it hit me: there were suddenly no single men anywhere.

A bunch of us stripped off and jumped into the hotel pool. Swigging from a bottle of champagne, I started thinking about Nathan. He had been kind and loving, and I had been blind. As the hazy sunrise opened up the sky I picked up my gold and white dress that I'd discarded like a shiny snakeskin by the pool's edge, and stumbled back to my room. I tried to recall why I'd ever left Nathan, but now I couldn't even remember.

I stayed on in Thailand after the others left. Jemima and her new husband lived in a big open house by the ocean and I set myself up in their spare room while they were on their honeymoon, writing in my diary, reading *War and Peace* and going for long walks along the beach. I had lots of time to reflect. I felt like I was in self-imposed rehab from all my past lives. New York had been heady and electrifying, but also stressful—I'd lived each day in a heightened state of survival, every minute precious and filled with urgency. Now, with time stretching out in front of me endlessly and with no plans of what to do next, my mind was empty and open to anything. All those years earlier when I'd been on antidepressants, just after Reuben, my brain had been forced to recline as if on a deck chair and watch my thoughts as they passed by. My failures, my fears: they had still hurt, but in the pleasant pharmaceutical fog I was able to let them float by instead of grasping onto them and letting them take over. I had no doubt the drugs had saved me, numbed my mind at a time when I'd just needed to get back on my feet, but once I'd started to feel more together I resented feeling so disembodied each day.

I thought I could just go cold turkey but it ended up taking over a year to get off them. When I finally did I was terrified by the prospect of having to live again with the everyday cawing of a crow in my ear, the relentless squawk of my own brain. But I discovered I could ignore it by staying very busy, blocking out the noise as effectively as the meds did with the band, with work, with relationships. But out here, with the blue-green water lapping at my ankles, I could hear my mind again loud and clear like those pre-Reuben days, and I was surprised by my own willingness to sit down with it and have a good chat. The conversations weren't as bad or as scary as I'd always feared. My brain and I were making peace with each other.

I celebrated turning twenty-eight with Jemima in the dirt courtyard of a small restaurant with a feast of som tam and khao pad. A bright green pandan birthday cake decorated with my name on it was brought out. I'd never had a cake with my name on it before. As I blew out the candles, I felt light and happy. Everything here seemed simple. A birthday was a cake. A day was a book and a swim.

At the markets I was drawn to beautiful fabrics, and bartered enthusiastically with stallholders for tablecloths, bed linen, wall hangings and candlesticks, wondering when I had got so into homewares. As I was haggling over a set of napkin holders, it hit me: I was building myself a trousseau. For the house I didn't have, but for which I suddenly pined feverishly.

The house I'd built with Jack all those years ago seemed like a doll's house on reflection, something we played in as children. Now, I wanted my own home. If I build it, maybe he will come, I thought. Who the 'he' was I was thinking of, I didn't know yet.

When you're single, well-meaning people and women's magazines always tell you that when you really know yourself you'll be ready to meet the love of your life. If this was true, I had work to do. I still couldn't stop thinking about the past: lost loves, lost careers, lost lives. One evening in my room, with the trumpety, joyous clamour of the Thai festival Songkran drifting through my open window from out on the street, I was transferring the wedding photos onto my laptop when the computer crashed. I lost everything—all my music and all my photos. I took a deep breath and decided to be calm and matter-of-fact about it. Zen. I told myself, *Well, I wanted to start all over again anyway, and now my past is erased so I really can.* Just like wearing the gold and white dress, the idea felt very un-me, but surprisingly, it fit. It made me feel excited.

I decided to enrol in a meditation course at a temple in Chiang Mai. On the overnight train with my yoga mat and backpack, warm air and bugs flew into my face through the broken window. I kept fidgeting with the ring I'd bought from a market stall where I'd been entranced by a jeweller bending and twisting metal into rings in front of us. I rarely wore jewellery, but I loved this ring. It was too big and fit only on my index finger, but the pastel colours and pentagonal shape of the stones reminded me of something talismanic. I bought it. On the train, I kept taking it off and putting it on my ring finger, letting it balance with my hand held still, pretending it belonged there. I tried to imagine what it would feel like to always wear it there. It calmed my nerves and made me feel peaceful and certain. I recognised the sensation—it felt right.

At the temple, no talking was allowed. We went to bed at eight o'clock every night, sleeping on a concrete floor with no mattresses, just two blankets spread out underneath each of us. We woke before sunrise, ate breakfast and then fasted until the following day. We weren't allowed to read or write, because that would take us away from the real work of mindfulness: the art of living in the present. I threw myself into the rules and discipline of the temple. I found solace in having all choices taken away from me, having to be somewhere at a specific time, being told what to do.

The course was filled with mostly older people, people from many different countries who seemed to be having mid-life crises, but there was one girl about my age. Whenever she padded in lightly, usually late, across the meditation room, I heard the creak of the wooden floorboards and looked up and smiled at her. She always flashed back a sparkling grin that spoke of northern European countries I'd never been to.

On Sundays we were free to explore the grounds of the temples that filled with visiting tourists. I was sitting under a tree late one afternoon that had a sign beneath it declaring that it was related to the actual Bodhi tree Siddhartha was sitting under when he achieved enlightenment. I was trying to get my head around that, when the sparkly girl came up to me and pulled me by the arm. Without saying a word, she dragged me to the tiny store in the tourist part of the temple and we bought ice-creams and took them to the lookout over the mountain. We ate them greedily as the sun set, giggling about breaking the rules, breaking the fast. It was my final night at the retreat, and I didn't care. Here, away from the monks, we talked quietly. Her name was Felicia and she was Swedish; the rhythm of her English delighted me. Her voice was husky, her accent espe-cially interesting when spoken in an illicit whisper. We rapidly updated each other on our lives, and after so many days of not speaking it felt so good. I was surprised at how swiftly I could sum up the last decade of my life. When I finished, she said: 'Well, I've been watching you. You seem really happy!'

I was surprised. 'Yeah,' I said slowly. 'I think I am.' Then with a careful pause: 'But I think I'm back in love with my ex-boyfriend.' I was shocked to hear myself say this out loud, but as the days of silence had worn on, from out of nowhere thoughts of Nathan had been flowering inside my mind like unexpected bursts of colour that now bunched together in one beautiful posy of absolute certainty.

From far off a thunderstorm had been rolling in. Felicia and I sat on rocks and from the top of the mountain we watched the lightning illuminate the city below us. The scattered lights of the houses blazed prettily like sequins as clean tears of radiance ripped through the sky, flashing bands, long strips glittering and sharp like metal. When the first drops of rain started, it felt beautiful, and in my daze I felt anointed, baptised. We were both silent, but it wasn't because of the rules.

I lay awake all night and fantasised about getting married. I could see it clearly: the dress, the garden setting, the circular tables laid with lace tablecloths. I'd make all the men wear suits and all the ladies wear white gloves. I'd never dreamt up my wedding before, even when I was a little kid, but the idea suddenly seemed so lovely: two people becoming a family. I couldn't sleep; there was too much to organise. I kept thinking about all the variables: who we would invite, what would be on the menu. But who the groom should be seemed at last fixed in my mind. It should be Nathan.

The next day before I left, one of the monks sprinkled water over my head and tied a white string of cotton around my wrist. 'Concentration. Happiness!' he said, blessing me with those qualities. I felt my face light up. Everything was so simple. I hugged Felicia goodbye. 'Safe travels back to home and love!' she beamed.

I caught a ride on the back of a truck down the mountain and then an overnight train back to Bangkok. At the station I hopped on a scooter with a stranger, my backpack sitting between his legs, and for the first time since arriving I didn't worry at all for my safety: I felt secure. When I got back to Jemima's house she and her husband were snuggled up on the sofa together watching a movie. I crept upstairs and called Nathan. It was late at night in Thailand, but in Australia it was daytime. We talked for two hours. He guided me through my computer problems and helped me locate my lost photos and music—they weren't gone after all, just hidden under some other file name. I felt like I was getting everything back. I told him I missed him and couldn't wait to see him when I got home to Australia, and he said like he always did, 'I miss you too.'

Coming back to Brisbane was a release, a freedom. It said to the world, I'm not trying anymore. I'd decided it was the right city to work in and pay back my travel debts, and try to practise what the monk had said to me: Concentration. Happiness.

I moved into a baby blue house near the river with Anna and Amy. Someone gave me an old futon and I set it up in my sunny new bedroom. I inherited a clothes rack and went about loading it up, surrounding myself with all the clothes from my parents' house. I overfilled it as always, until it was teetering. The Fender Telecaster I'd bought in New York sat in the corner of my bedroom with my tiny practice amp, and I placed some incense and candles on my bedside table. I sat on my futon on the floor and called Nathan.

Over the next few weeks, our phone calls became a regular, beautiful ritual. We didn't talk about anything in particular, just TV shows and music and what we'd been doing, but I could feel us getting closer to each other like we used to be.

I got in touch with my old publishing contacts and was offered a freelance editing job. Things were coming together; it was like I belonged and had never left this small, easy, sunshiney city. I jogged every afternoon as the sun set in pinks and purples over the river snaking through the city and out again. I'd stop by the edge to stretch, and get lost staring at the movement of the water. Whenever I thought I had worked out the rhythm and direction of the gentle waves, they'd switch. I never knew which way they'd go.

As much as I wanted my own house to live in, being back in a sharehouse with girls who were just like me made it feel like a family. Anna and Amy and I turned the wobbly timber

Queenslander into a peaceful haven. We nurtured succulents from mini watering cans, collected crockery and silver spoons from jumble sales, wore feathers in our hair, bought vases secondhand and filled them with flowers we picked from other people's gardens. We did hand sewing in front of the TV and lined record sleeves along our window sills, forgetting to take the records out first so they got warped by the sun. We cut our own hair, grew tomatoes and basil, wore brooches, baked cupcakes, owned rabbits and kittens, invited people round for picnics under beach umbrellas in our backyard, bought strappy shoes from op shops that never fit us, turned milk crates into coffee tables, took painting classes, pulled pillows out onto the nature strip and read in the afternoon sun. In our late twenties, having all imagined such days were past, our girlishness blossomed again like the blush on a just-kissed cheek.

I started writing every day on a personal blog, just to get into the habit again, trying on the idea of being a writer. I looked forward to waking up and deciding what to write that day. Some days I spent hours on it. At first, I didn't tell anyone—it was a secret. Anna and Amy were busy working on their writing projects too. Some mornings we were all locked away in our rooms and every now and then I looked up from what I was doing to hear the tap-tap-tapping of keyboards in symphony through the thin walls and it gave me such a feeling of rightness. Concentration equalled happiness.

One night Nathan phoned to tell me he was coming to Brisbane for work and I was awoken out of my happy domestic and writing reverie. This was my chance. It would be the first time that we'd actually seen each other since that awful lunch in New York. I bought flowers and vacuumed. I planned to take him out to a beautiful dinner. I was going to surprise him and tell him that I was in love with him again. He'd stay the night, and then we would get married and have babies. That night I woke up to a crash. I switched on the light, still half-asleep. The clothes rack had fallen down. All my dresses lay in a heap. I let them stay like that and went back to sleep.

The next morning just before Nathan was due to arrive, I checked my email. In the instant it took to skim-read three lines from an old friend, I felt all the certainty and confidence I'd been building up fall away. A girl I'd lived with years ago for a short time in Melbourne had killed herself. We weren't close friends, but I'd shared so many small moments with her in our sharehouse. Books we had read, learning how we liked our tea, making a cup for each other whenever we boiled the kettle without needing to ask. The scent of the bathroom after her shower, the steamy air saturated with her grapefruit moisturiser. I hadn't seen her in a couple of years and I knew she'd been through some really tough times, but I hadn't been expecting this.

I heard the cab pull up and Nathan knocked on the door. We sat opposite each other at a Thai restaurant. The food was different to what I had eaten in Thailand—it didn't taste as fresh and it was so expensive. I moved it round on my plate. Nathan tried to talk, to make it lighter and easier, but I couldn't concentrate on him, I couldn't hear him. I tried to focus on his eyes, always kind and interested, and keep up with all the stuff he was telling me about, all the stuff that had happened in Melbourne since I'd been away. But I felt no connection to that place anymore and I just felt far away, from him and from everything. As we walked home silently through the park, his hand took mine. I tried to untangle my feelings. I wasn't sure what I wanted now. It had been easier to know when I was far away, with the lightning flashing across the mountains and all the lights and the people and the rest of the world far off in the distance.

I pushed aside the pile of clothes that had fallen down the night before to make room on the futon for him. He asked me if I wanted to talk about her, so I did, but I kept trailing off and getting confused. I couldn't work out why I felt so sad. Nathan had always been a good listener, but now it was making me feel crazy to hear myself. I felt like I was being over the top, a drama queen; I had really only known her as a passerby, for a short time. I couldn't understand my own feelings and I got more and more irritated. When he tried to hug me I felt myself go cold. I pushed him away. We went to sleep, our bodies not touching at all.

Twenty-nine

Grandma and Grandpa lived in Toowoomba, in the neat part of town that brimmed with mowed lawns, flowerbeds and churches. Grandpa was a POW, a veteran who had been imprisoned at Changi during World War II. He had always been unwell as a result, but now in his eighties he was frailer than ever. When he was out, he wore a badge pinned to his collar that said 'VIP—Visually Impaired Person'. Grandma was his full-time carer day and night but she suffered from various ailments too: she'd had tuberculosis as a young woman and had had part of her lung removed. Ever since my mum could remember they had both been telling everyone they were going to die tomorrow, but they were still here.

Grandma usually pepped up when I asked her to tell me stories about her family. She was the youngest of seven children, four girls and three boys, and as a kid I loved poring over the photos of the sisters determinedly dressed in smart tailored suits and stockings, even though it was the Depression and they didn't have much money.

Sometimes she didn't want to talk about the past though, and I wondered if sometimes memories were more than the entertaining stories you told over a cup of tea and Arnott's biscuits: maybe some people preferred not to treasure them. I crept away to the spare room at the back of the house where I'd found her old scrapbooks packed away in a cupboard, and got my stories anyway. The scrapbooks were fascinating; they were full of newspaper clippings stuck onto old butcher's paper like a child's careful school project. My favourite one was the scrapbook dedicated to her adventurous middle sister, my great-aunt Daphne. Daphne was unmarried and independent; the family described her as 'the one who got away' because she had escaped her small town with its conservative, constrained life. Rejecting numerous suitors, she had gone travelling on her own to exotic countries. This was the early fifties, and I studied the studio portrait of her that hung in my grandparents' house, admiring her strong features and her patrician nose; she gazed far-off away in the distance as if she could see something outside the frame that we couldn't. If I got up close enough the shiny glass reflected my own face back to me and I wished my features matched up to hers, that I resembled her even a tiny bit. But I didn't. When it was time to go I'd put the scrapbooks back in the cupboard, say goodbye to Grandma and promise to write, like I always did.

Grandma was my first penpal.

Ever since I was little she wrote to me, letters that described her most recent illnesses and Toowoomba's Carnival of Flowers shows in equally colourful detail. Her handwriting always looked like it had been written with a spirograph. Every year on my birthday she sent twenty dollars in an old-fashioned birthday card and one of her letters. As I got older, although the sum of money didn't change the writing did, growing a bit more crooked every year. Then on my twenty-ninth birthday she didn't send a letter but just a hundred dollars in a birthday card, signing it simply 'Love Grandma and Grandpa'. It was so much money, more than they'd ever sent before. I wanted to spend it on something meaningful so I went to the bookshop and bought the complete set of Proust's *In Search of Lost Time*, haggling for a discount because I was buying all seven volumes at once.

I'd spent the whole year back in Brisbane, working to pay off my travel debts, and then saving up so I could leave again. I had read a lofty quote somewhere that 'travelling allows you to explore undiscovered continents within yourself',

and I had fallen in love with that idea. I was feeling rest-
less again. When my brother moved to India on a teaching
contract I decided this would be the perfect escape. I would
go and stay with him for six months and read Proust.

I flew into Mumbai and Lachy picked me up, towering
above the crowd of other men outside the airport who hollered
and waved at me for attention. He grabbed my arm, steering
me through the swarm of people to the car he'd organised.
We drove two hours through a steamy, denim blue morning to
his apartment in Pune. The school he worked at had put him
up in a two-bedroom penthouse within a 'society'—apartment
blocks that surrounded a small garden and swimming pool.
Armed guards peered out from under their hats when we drove
through the gates and then waved us through. I looked over
at Lachy. He had grown an elaborate handlebar moustache.
My brother, now a 27-year-old man, was a mystery to me.
Growing up, I had always resented him: I thought he'd been
spoilt because he was the only son and a star athlete. While
Xanthe and Analiese and I had one shelf of trophies between
us—for netball and athletics and dancing—he had an entire
wall dedicated to his sports trophies. He and I always bick-
ered and fought, and it was only after I'd gone to Turkey and
left him, the only kid still at home with Mum and Dad, that
we started to view each other as potential allies. By the time I
got back we had stopped straight-out detesting each other, but

we had still never really hung out as adults. But as I settled into my new life in Pune, we got into a routine of sitting on the balcony every evening, drinking Bombay Sapphire and lemonade and watching the sun turn pink. And as we talked, the mystery of him and how he'd come to be a teacher in India, instead of an Olympian, unravelled. I'd never bothered to ask him until now about why he'd never become the sportsman he'd been destined to be. I'd always thought that he'd stopped running in his twenties because he got distracted by girls and partying. Every weekend as a kid he'd competed in surf life saving events and athletics carnivals. He was always in the newspaper for sporting achievements and by the time he was nineteen we were all convinced he was on his way to competing at the 2000 Sydney Olympics. That same year, he competed in the World Surf Life Saving Championships in Hawaii and noticed a sharp pain in his calves. He came back and ran his personal-best time at an athletics meet, winning the hundred-metre sprint, but with the pain becoming unrelenting he had to take a break.

It turned out he never ran again. One night on our Pune balcony overlooking a dirt road and distant pastures filled with cows, hearing the end-of-day traffic honking past, he told me why. He had discovered he had a rare condition called popliteal artery entrapment syndrome. He described the condition as 'the evil twin brother of shin splints'—it meant that he was born with a tendon cutting off an artery behind his knees, which explained why each time he ran he felt an aching and throbbing in his knees and legs. I struggled to understand. 'But,' I protested, 'running was your entire life.'

'It's just the way it is. The doctors wouldn't operate because my life wasn't threatened by it,' he said quietly. With a sigh and the ice clinking gently in his glass, he added, 'I never felt like I was really a sportsperson anyway.'

'Are you serious?' I almost squealed at the absurdity of it. 'That's exactly who you are—it's who you've been since you were three years old!'

'Yeah, but what can you do,' he shrugged. It seemed so crazy and tragic to me, to be so talented at something and not get to do it. The biggest challenge was trying to find out what you were good at in the first place: that's what I'd observed with my friends, anyway. So many of us in our twenties were still just trying to figure that out. But Lachy had known what he was good at when he was in primary school, and now he wasn't able to do it. It seemed grossly unfair. His acceptance of that filled me with sorrow. I didn't know what to say so I went inside and topped up our drinks.

I loved India. Everything seemed simple, uncomplicated, because it was a fresh start again. Whenever I went to a new place I always felt there was no pressure to be something or someone, so I could be anyone. I thrived on it.

Shut inside the high walls, neighbours peering out to stare at me over their balconies, made me feel like I was back in Turkey. Except it wasn't Turkey; now I could look after myself. Ten years on, I was more confident: a woman. If anyone stared I stared straight back at them until they looked away.

Every morning, I jogged around the compound. No one else seemed to exercise in public. Women in saris sweeping their balconies peered down at me curiously. At first I was self-conscious in my shorts and T-shirt, but I shook off the feeling. Not knowing anyone else there made me feel free. The garden was circular and only about a hundred metres circumference, so I ran round and round it to get the kilometres in, ducking my head under low-lying fronds as Prince pumped through my headphones.

After my jog I ran up the twenty-one floors to our apartment. I made porridge with nuts and fresh papaya every morning, took a shower and started work. Work meant writing every day on my blog that I'd started in Brisbane. After I'd done that, the afternoon had cooled down and I could at last open up the French doors. I'd take *In Search of Lost Time* out to the balcony and as the call to prayer sounded I sunk contentedly into the flowery world of early twentieth-century France.

Lachy went to work at his school every day and by the time he got home at night I'd cooked a delicious Indian dinner using the vegetables and spices I had discovered at the local market. I kept house. Swept a lot. There was always so much dust.

On weekends, we went out in a rickshaw to run errands. Lachy's head almost touched the top of the canvas roof, so he had to sit hunched over, like our dad in the tiny Escort he drove for years, a lanky casualness, knobbly knees always getting in the way. The footpaths were narrow and crowded, and everyone walked along on the streets where rickshaws would hurtle by and almost knock us all over. I bought fabrics from tailors and got some of my favourite dresses copied. It was a major discovery for me: this way I could hold on to my dresses even as they developed rips and tears and became unwearable. I was replicating the pieces I loved and refused to let go of; I would wear them forever by hook or by crook.

Lachy was going back to Australia for his school holidays. I would stay on in Pune alone. 'Will you be all right?' he asked.

'Of course!' I told him.

I had six weeks all on my own. It was now deep in monsoon season; the weather was too hot and wet to leave the house.

I swam in the pool in the early mornings before the kids filled it with bomb dives, and then drank vodka sundowners on the balcony as the rain moved across the sky. I let my red-dyed hair grow out to its natural colour, the dark wispy blonde pushing through so it looked like I had grey hair emerging. I embraced the feeling I had of being a spinster, a woman alone. Thinking about Great-Aunt Daphne I felt content, strong, happy. I sat on a mat on the tiled floor, the room full of sunlight, underlining sentences of Proust. I was up to the third volume, *The Guermantes Way*, where Marcel's grandma dies after an ordinary carriage ride one afternoon down the Champs-Élysées. I found myself underlining almost every sentence.

We make a point of telling ourselves that death can come at any moment, but when we do so we think of that moment as something vague and distant, not as something that can have anything to do with the day that has already begun or might mean that death— or the first sign of its partial possession of us, after which it will never loosen its hold again—will occur this afternoon, the almost inevitable afternoon with its hourly activities prescribed in advance.

The more time I spent alone, the more I wanted to be alone. Gradually, I started to not want to leave the house at all;

I dreaded even the smallest errand to the market. At night, tiny birds settled in under the alcoves of our building, sitting swollen in the cracks, scuttling to hold on. The sound their claws made was like someone trying to get in. I kept checking to make sure the front door was locked. I could always hear people out in the hall. The noise of the families next door, the unfamiliar closeness of apartment living, started to frighten me. I'm safe, I reassured myself. I'm safe.

About once a week the electricity went out and I had to use candles. During those times the noises were even louder; there was shouting on the streets, shuffling in the hallway, and I didn't dare go out of the apartment, even when I needed water.

A couple of weeks before Lachy returned, I decided enough was enough. I felt like I was wasting this opportunity—I needed to get out and see more of India. I organised to meet up in Delhi with a girl I knew from Brisbane, Mina, and stay with her relatives. Mina met me at the airport to take me to her uncle and aunt's house. On the way a cricket ball bounced through our rickshaw and out the other side as we were moving. 'What are the chances of that happening?!' I cried. I looked behind me in astonishment, back to the kids who had been playing cricket. 'It was going so fast that if it had hit your head, you would have been killed,' said Mina soberly.

We took a train to Agra to see the Taj Mahal. It was beautiful, every detail carved in memory of this precious loved one, a scrapbook in stone that would never fade or curl up at the corners.

Mina was ten years younger than me. This was her first trip overseas. I felt like the wiser, older, well-travelled chaperone or aunt out of an E.M. Forster novel. I told her we *had* to go to Varanasi, with its ghats and death ceremonies. Bodies burning, the smoke, the water. But because of the stifling heat, we decided that first we should head north, to the cool mountains of Darjeeling to refresh. We planned to visit for just a few days, but we loved it so much we ended up staying for two weeks. It was picturesque. Pots of pink flowers bloomed on windowsills and narrow dirt streets twisted steeply up and down the hillside. In the mornings the fog lifted from the mountains like a curtain rising at the start of a play. We strolled through tea paddies and were offered little tastes of tea in miniature paper cups. It was a relief to not be sweating all the time, choked by heat. But it got so cold at night we had to buy beanies and thick knitted socks from the market stalls.

One night we were sitting in a small local bar and two American guys started to chat to Mina. I watched, their eyes fixed completely on her. Eventually, one of them started politely trying to make conversation with me, but I couldn't think of anything to say. I had been on my own for so long, I didn't feel like just talking about movies and places I'd been to. It seemed like a lot of energy to give someone I'd never see again, so I went home to read.

I bought a postcard for my grandma at a market stall and wrote to her while I sat in a restaurant overlooking the distant Himalayan peaks. I told her about Darjeeling, about how fit I was getting walking around because wherever you went you had to go up or down a hill. I signed it 'Love, Lorelei' like I always did, and put the postcard in my jeans pocket to take to the post office the next day before we left. That night, the fog curled its villain's moustache around the mountains.

By morning the rain was so heavy all the roads were bogged. An earthquake in Bangladesh had triggered land-slides that poured down the mountains, crushing houses, jeeps and people as far away as here in Darjeeling. Our land-lady said there was no way we'd be getting out today.

The rain fell for three days and Mina and I were shut indoors, becoming ever more tense and starting to bicker out of frustration. On the fourth day, we trudged through the mud to the ticket office to try to change the dates on our train tickets, but were told there were no more seats for at least a fortnight. We could see some jeeps were going around the roadblocks and decided to try our luck. We sought out a driver and paid him double to get us out of there. Throwing our backpacks on the back seat of his small red hatchback we tumbled in. A cross dangled crookedly from the rear-view mirror, and a plastic buddha sat placidly on the dashboard. Coffee-coloured streams of mud gushed past us as we drove slowly down the mountain. Everyone had the same idea as us, and there was a pile-up of traffic. As we crept along behind a line of jeeps, I could see small rocks breaking free from the cliffsides, falling in clusters like autumn leaves. Goats were trapped in the mud, bleating. Fragments of cloth in the distance, which might have been attached to people, stood out like flags amid the dirt-swamped colour of everything else. We passed a truck coming the other way; it had GOOD LUCK painted on the front.

The traffic had come to a complete stop and the driver got out to see what was happening. Mina and I sat in the car, the rain pelting down. The driver walked around the corner, and disappeared for over an hour. We were starting to freak out. Mina turned to me, her eyes big and frightened. 'What should we do?' I was used to being the older one, the chaperone who always knew the location of the entrance to the bus station and at which restaurant to eat, but I had lost confidence. I was scared. 'Well, I guess the car seems the safest place to be,' she said sensibly after I didn't answer, and I was grateful she had made a decision for us.

When the driver finally returned, he shrugged his shoulders and told us there was no way out today. He turned the car around and drove us slowly back to Darjeeling.

We were lucky to get the last two beds in town for the night, at a small and run-down bed and breakfast. We hung our damp clothes over the bedpost to dry near the open fire. I was freezing. The power had gone out so we used candles for extra light. We were muddy but it was too freezing to have cold showers, so we just splashed icy water on our faces and zipped up early into our sleeping bags. I bunched myself up into the smallest, warmest ball I could and tried to forget about everything until morning.

It was sunny when we woke. Walking outside we saw rubbish strewn everywhere, like a tide had gone out. Locals were assessing the flood damage to their houses, and like flowers unfolding with the sun, one by one restaurants opened again for business. We ordered a last breakfast of banana pancakes, and I went to see if the post office was open yet. It wasn't. The card I wrote to my grandma was crusted with dried mud and I tucked it back into my jeans pocket.

I didn't feel ready to go home. I wanted to stay on the road. Some other tourists we'd met had told me that Kolkata was interesting and colonially charming, so while Mina decided to go back to Delhi, where she could sleep and recuperate and pretend she wasn't really in India, I chose Kolkata, of which the only thing I knew was Mother Teresa. Mina and I said goodbye with the briefest hug and jumped in separate jeeps because they were filling up quickly, my familiar companion suddenly vanishing into the distance as my jeep lurched down the mountain. I was suddenly overwhelmed with regret. Although the last few days had been fraught, I had loved travelling with Mina. Sharing rooms, meals and books with her for two weeks had been fun, and now she had disappeared so suddenly I felt a sense of loneliness brewing that was unlike the aloneness I had sought to cultivate back in Pune. It was the difference between choosing to be on your own and not consciously choosing it; discovering it had just happened anyway.

At the bottom of the mountain I transferred onto a bus. I was assigned a seat at the very back, by the window, with eight other people crammed onto the same bench. I asked the man who was squashed up close next to me to change seats with the woman who appeared to be a family member next to him. All I could think about was that the ride was ten hours long and we would be travelling overnight: I couldn't fall asleep with him sitting so close. I'd seen ladies-only carriages on trains in India and I thought the request was reasonable. But he seemed insulted. He shouted at me and refused to move. His hands were blistered and worn and I felt sorry for him, but I was tired and over it. I had got suspicious and mean, I knew it, and I didn't like it. But being on my own, I felt I had to be.

I thought of my great-aunt Daphne, travelling on a train through New Zealand in 1953. Were women more protected back then? And if so, did it make them feel more restricted or freer? I imagined a different world of etiquette, where dashing gentlemen would have offered to help with her luggage. How would she have known whom to trust? I wondered if she'd been sitting next to a man on that train trip.

I remembered exactly which carriage she was on because I had read it in the scrapbooks at Grandma's house. The first-class carriages were all at the back of the train, safe. The second-class seats were all at the front. It was Christmas Eve, and the Wellington–Auckland night express was moving through Tangiwai, on the north island, and was about to pass over the Whangaehu River. The driver didn't see that the bridge across the river had been swept away by volcanic mudflow from Mount Ruapehu. One hundred and fifty-one people died, mostly those in the front, second-class carriages, including Great-Aunt Daphne.

After her body had been recovered from the rushing, icy-cold river, Daphne's clothes had been folded neatly and sent back to her family in Australia, and when Grandma and her sisters opened the package, the overwhelming smell of sulphur emanated from them. I wished I'd thought to ask if they'd kept her clothes. I was thinking of that train, of the tracks that disappeared into nothingness, when the bus swung around a corner in the darkness and the man with the blistered hands fell onto me and woke up with a start. I lashed out at him in anger, waking everyone else on the bus, and huddled further into the smudged window, ashamed.

We arrived early the next morning. I hadn't slept. Kolkata was hot, much hotter than Darjeeling, but I was still shuddering from the cold and wind that had cut through me in the mountains so I didn't think to remove any layers I was wearing. The bus deposited me in front of a neat, verdant cricket ground. I got in one of the waiting cabs, too tired to haggle the price, and asked the driver to take me to the main backpacker quarter, Sudder Street. As we drove into town, the irritated outburst of the night before dissolved into familiar, positive feelings of excitement and discovery. Why, Kolkata was a delight! Such lavish green parks! Such elegant colonial architecture!

When I got out, hawkers swarmed around me, beckoning me to their restaurant, their hotel, their *there*. I tried to storm away and lose them but a new lethargy strangled my limbs. My backpack felt like a boulder. In an instant I knew that if I didn't find a place soon I would keel over right there on the street.

I followed a hawker to a hotel and banged my head on the threshold as I went in. It was dirty, small and windowless. I was feeling too dizzy and exhausted to look for anything else so I agreed to take the room. When I lay my head down on the pillow, I smelt the overpowering aroma of other people's scalps and it made me jolt upright again. Maybe I would feel better if I went for a walk. I headed back out into the steamy streets thinking I should try to change hotels, but the sun pushed itself into my temples and I couldn't think clearly. I wasn't feeling very hungry, but I hadn't eaten since lunch the previous day, so I went to a nearby restaurant and ordered a paratha and spicy dal. As I ate, I started sweating and my stomach churned. I managed only a few mouthfuls until I was overcome with a choking feeling. I paid the bill and walked slowly back to the room, having never felt this sick before.

The bathroom was grotty; a shower nozzle stuck out randomly from one of the walls, the floor doubling as a shower cubicle. There were cigarette stubs blocking the drain in the sink and the smell when I walked in instantly made me want to spew, and I did. I lay down on the floor but within a second I had to throw up again. I didn't make it to the toilet and hurled into the sink instead. I collapsed on the bathroom tiles.

I remembered Lachy would be back in Pune by now. I didn't want to worry him but I felt so miserable and I didn't know what else to do. I pulled myself up and found my phone, and pressed his number into it weakly with my index finger. He sprang into brotherly action immediately. He told me that my symptoms sounded like I was either severely dehydrated or food poisoned, and either way I should go back out to the street and buy two large bottles of water this minute, and mix one with the rehydration mixture he had packed in my bag, and alternate drinking both over the next few hours.

'But I can't walk!' I cried.

'You're going to have to,' he said. 'You have to get water. Right now.'

I only had to venture outside about fifty metres to a market stall, but by the time I got to the vendor I was crumpled up in pain. I pointed to two bottles of water, and then turned to the footpath and spewed. A man with enormous boils covering his entire body walked past. My spew missed his ankles by centimetres.

Onlookers gathered, the tall and lanky men who are generally found standing like public sculptures on every street in India, who suddenly form themselves into one massive, hulking organism whenever something of interest is happening on the streets. I felt as if I was performing a show for them.

The street vendor, from whom I was trying to buy the water, noticed where my vomit had landed and became agitated. Without either of us speaking a word of each other's language, he was able to communicate that I'd spewed in the wrong place, and that the ideal location was in fact a half-metre to the left of my original site, in the gutter next to the parked tyre of one of the shiny cabs. I remembered how, in Pune, I'd seen a rat nibbling at fresh vomit on the street, and I spewed again, this time, I knew from the vendor's encouraging murmurs, in the proper place.

Eyes downcast, struggling to carry the two litres of water, I shuffled back to the stuffy hotel room and made another phone call to Lachy, who, while I had been spewing out on the street, had booked me a plane ticket out of there. I just had to get myself to the airport the next day, he told me. I promised him I could, and passed out in relief, so grateful to have a brother.

The next morning I awoke with that surprise I get sometimes of still being alive. The painful stomach cramps persisted but I was spurred into action knowing I was going back to Pune. I reached down to the bottom of my backpack. I'd been wearing comfortable travelling gear the whole trip: jeans and long-sleeved blouses, a shawl around my shoulders. Excavating the contents of my bag, I found the only dress I'd brought from Lachy's place in Pune, rolled up so small I had forgotten about it. Thrown in just in case I got a dinner date: a hot photojournalist; a rugged geologist. The chiffon was completely crushed now, and it stank of the vanilla oil that had spilled through my bag. I gazed at it dizzily. Where had it even come from? It seemed like some luxury item from another world.

I'd first seen the dress, the colour of peacock feathers, in a vintage dress shop in Hahndorf, just outside Adelaide. It was chiffon with a silky lining that always felt cool and luxurious against my skin. I had been in Hahndorf, a German settlement, a touristy place marketed as a town where 'the past comes to life', for my cousin's wedding the year before. When I'd caught the bouquet Grandma turned to me cheekily and said, 'You're next, Lorelei!' and I laughed, but she turned suddenly serious. 'I might not make it if you don't hurry,' she said.

The dress was wrinkled, but clean. I pulled it on over my jeans and threw a shawl around my shoulders. I was so enervated from vomiting that it sagged, but the touch of it against my skin was a comfort. I could feel my hair was knotted; I didn't look in the mirror to check. The door slammed behind me.

I spent the flight crumpled against the window of the plane with headphones in and sunglasses on, my eyes squeezed shut. I tried not to think about how I'd read in the newspapers that this domestic airline had a history of crashing. Lachy was at the airport when I landed and had a rickshaw waiting. He rushed over and threaded his arm through mine to help me walk. I was bent over like an old woman.

'Jeez, you look terrible,' Lachy said. 'C'mon, you old grandma,' he added jovially, helping me up into the rickshaw. He handed me a bottle of water and I sipped at it.

The ride was bumpy; from out of nowhere I thought of Proust, which I hadn't opened for days; about how you never expect death to come before your carriage has reached the Champs-Élysées.

Lachy had been having dinner with friends at a restaurant we always ate at, the German Bakery, and left them to come and pick me up. A few months later a bomb would go off there, killing seventeen people, many of them tourists. By that time I had left India, but Lachy hadn't, and the night it happened he decided not to eat there on a whim. He instead chose another restaurant a few metres away and heard it happen, saw people running away, bloodied and terrified.

We were riding along and Lachy was talking, his voice shouting above the motor of the rickshaw. 'You know, you always exaggerate things and make everything seem so dramatic, so on the phone I didn't know if you were putting it on. But yeah—look at you. This time you're actually really sick.'

The rickshaw sped along and I held onto Lachy's arm, feeling like I might fall out. When we got home I hobbled to my room. I unpeeled my jeans and the unsent postcard fell out of the pocket. I got into the lumpy bed, smoothed my good dress out over my knees and fell asleep with the silk lining against my skin, thinking there was something I had to do for my grandma; she might not make it if I didn't hurry.

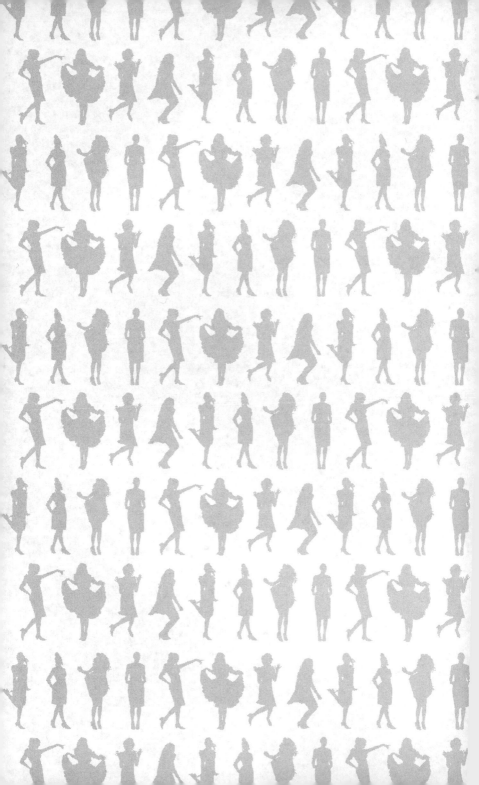

Thirty

I love seeing photos of Mum as a young woman, wearing all the dresses she made that I still own. I also love that she can whip up incredible meals using anything that's in the cupboard, the way she hangs art round the house, the way she sticks memo notes and movie posters and reminders on the fridge, creates an expressive mosaic, arresting and full of colour. She once told me that, like many women her age, she genuinely hadn't known what to do with her life except have kids—it simply hadn't occurred to her to do anything else. So she had the four of us. Later on when she had more time she realised she wanted other things too, so she'd gone back to university. But she'd never finished her teaching diploma. When I was older I became aware of how frustrating it had been for her, how she had longed for other things, a more artistic life perhaps. She seemed resigned to it now. She loved her family and brought her artistic sensibilities to how she raised us kids, but it made me sad to think about how she might have had a career doing something equally fulfilling if she'd had the chance or the confidence. Mum had always been the most creative person I knew, and the older I got the more I wanted to be exactly like her and yet nothing like her.

I didn't realise thirty was a deadline until I was a few months out from it. It was then that I tuned into something, I didn't even know where it came from, some vibration or message from movies and magazines and books and music that suggested the end of your twenties was a milestone and you should make sure you have something to show for it. Sighting thirty from so near by was a shock, like a piece of land I'd been sailing towards for a long time and quite abruptly when it was in front of me I had an urge to turn back. It was suddenly crucial to not have any regrets. Unlike my mum, I didn't want to look back on my own decisions and realise there were things I had always wanted that I hadn't tried.

When I was in high school I had auditioned to play one of the main roles in the school musical *Bye Bye Birdie*, but I was given a chorus role instead. It was a small speaking role, just two lines, as one of the schoolgirls' mums, a straight-laced character called Mrs Merkel, who—during the final performance—I decided to transform, at the last minute, into a Mrs Robinson.

'Yoo hoo! Conrad!' I purred as I made my entrance. Leaning sultrily against the wobbly doorframe, I pulled down the sleeve of my dress to reveal a bare shoulder to Conrad Birdie, the handsome young rockstar all the teenagers were in love with. I was sixteen, and had a flush of joy when I was doing it. It felt like something Liza Minelli would do, or Barbra Streisand in *Funny Girl*. I thought everyone would laugh and see the genius in turning a tightly wound fifties schoolmarm into a seductress. But there were probably a hundred people in the audience and as I listened, waiting for a reaction, all I heard was stony silence.

After a shocked pause from my fellow performers, the show went on.

No one mentioned it to me afterwards; not the director or the students or any of the parents. I wasn't sure if they just hadn't noticed, or if they were pretending it hadn't happened because they were embarrassed for me. The idea had felt good when I was thinking it up, convincing myself that for the final performance I was really going to show the school community what I had. I felt they'd overlooked my talent by not giving me a major role. But as I stared out into the darkness of the silent auditorium, lit up on the stage, my costume still hanging off the shoulder, all I wanted was to disappear. So ever since Mrs Merkel, I had been scared to find out whether I had been overlooked, or whether I was just a really bad actor. The likelihood of hearing the stony silence again after I'd said my line had always been too ghastly to imagine, but now I had to know.

So I decided to audition for NIDA, the National Institute of Dramatic Art, where Cate Blanchett had studied, to find out once and for all if I was an actor so I could either pursue it or put the idea to bed forever. I threw myself into study, shrugging off the niggling feeling that most of the people auditioning with me would be teenagers straight out of high school. I was determined to not feel like I was too old and too late—my mum might have felt that way at sixty, but that was all the more reason to feel that, at almost thirty, I still had time to find the thing I was good at. I read play after play and studied my sisters' old acting textbooks: *How to Audition* and *How to Play Shakespeare*. I stuck a quote from the actor John Barrymore on my wall: 'You can only be as good as you're prepared to be bad.' This, to me, was the essence of it. I had to be brave enough to be bad in order to potentially discover I was good. In the back of my mind there was always the possibility that I might even be great, and that the audience at *Bye Bye Birdie* had been wrong.

I bought a book of lectures that had been given by Stella Adler, an acting coach who studied with Stanislavski before establishing the Conservatory of Acting in New York in 1949. Her lectures teased apart the plays I was reading and helped me understand them: Chekhov, Ibsen and Strindberg. Reading the book it felt as if Stella was sitting beside me. The text of her lectures was interspersed with baffled students' interjections; I imagined kids in horn-rimmed glasses being cut down to size by this woman with the pin curls and a glass of wine balancing next to her on the lectern. She had died twenty years earlier but Stella became my guru, not just for acting but for everything. I sat on the verandah at Mum and Dad's house, looking up often to dream out into the distance, across the trees to the ocean. 'When you study acting, you study how to live life,' she wrote.

Flashes came back to me about how I had behaved in the past. The things I'd done and the words I'd spoken. I remembered how hidden I was when I was with Reuben, and the lines I'd spoken dramatically when I'd tried to express my need for him. I thought of trying to hold onto the band when we were all splitting off into our own directions, how hard it had always been for me to accept that things ended. I thought of how much I had known it would hurt Nathan in New York when I told him I'd moved on, but how I'd done it anyway. And then how when I decided I wanted him, he wasn't there anymore. Were they my words from inside me or just lines of dialogue I'd absorbed over the years—from films, books and plays—and parroted back in to my real world? Had I really felt these moments, were they true? What was my character?

'In your choice lies your talent,' Stella said. 'Make good choices.' Now I wondered how much of what had happened had been my choice, and how much had I just let happen.

I paid my sister Xanthe to give me professional acting lessons. She taught drama at school, and worked alongside her husband Sam in community theatre. Both performed regularly in shows; theatre was their life. So, once a week I went to their house where their toddler Poppy sat and watched while Xanthe coached me through my monologues. One evening Sam told me he had auditioned for NIDA a couple of times and had got through to the final rounds twice. It was impressive.

'Well, I don't expect to get in, I'm just doing it to see,' I said flippantly.

'With that approach, you probably actually will get in,' Sam said. I was secretly pleased. I loved the idea that I might be the unexpected dark horse who would suddenly reveal all this surprising talent to the world. I wanted to get in even more now.

I selected a monologue from *Wild Honey*, which was adapted from a play by Chekhov, and a contemporary piece from a play called *The Seed*. But my most challenging monologue was my Shakespeare pick: Cleopatra. Regal and strong, yet vulnerable and human. Cleopatra! The first time I read her lines I swooned at the beauty of the language. I had to concentrate to understand its meaning at first but once I did, each sentence transported me. My mum was unsure. 'Do you really think you can do Cleopatra?' she asked timidly. 'It's a big role.'

'Of course I can,' I snapped. 'You have no idea what I can do.'

Stella said, 'Every character wants something. You just have to find out what it is.' But I was realising that just finding it could take a long time. Maybe some people never do, or if they do they are foiled from following it through.

I'd recently heard from Lachy in India, who'd sent me some songs he'd written. He was also taking beautiful photographs, training his eye to see colour and texture, and painting as well. I had felt so sorry for him since our conversation, about the end of his athletics career, but since then he had quietly cultivated other dreams, and the result was stunning: artwork that had all the more richness to it for having to be dug up from deep beneath more surface layers of ambition. It inspired me. I had lashed out at Mum for doubting my ability to play Cleopatra, but I could hear in her voice that the insecurity was hers, not mine. I was more confident about this than I'd ever been.

Cate Blanchett was playing the role of Blanche in *A Streetcar Named Desire* in Sydney, and my friends Ben and Scott and I flew down with all our mums to see it. We sat right at the back in one long row, chattering excitedly before the curtain went up, so thrilled to watch her perform in real life. Having only ever seen her in films we were besotted by this idea of seeing her act just for a roomful of people, just for us.

From the moment she walked out onstage I found myself holding my breath, hoping desperately she would be good, that she would do well. I was nervous for her: did she know we were here, that we had come all this way and that we loved her? We were sitting near the back of the theatre but with her movements and her voice she pushed herself up and out towards us, and she didn't feel far away at all.

Early on in the first act, we noticed a murmuring from the row in front of us. It was soft at first, and then suddenly shrill. I looked over to see a young woman prodding the elderly lady next to her who had melted into the chair, her head lolling slightly to the side. 'Mum?' she said softly, followed by more of a shriek: 'Mum!'

The actors on the stage looked up briefly. They kept going with their lines, but there was a flicker of acknowledgement, unmistakable in their longer pauses and their slightly altered tones, that something wasn't right back here. The audience sat still in their seats, all the usual weight-shifting of bodies and staccato coughs on hold. We were sitting right behind but because it was dark we couldn't clearly see what was happening. The woman in front of us was in a panic now, shaking her mum's shoulders and speaking to her in a measured, intense tone, trying to wake her. Audience members who were seated closer to the stage were craning their necks to see what was going on.

An usher arrived and shone the torch at the women, before disappearing and coming back with a bottle of water as the commotion spread down the rows of people. I heard a random audience member hiss sharply: 'Get an ambulance!' The people in the row where it was all happening pushed themselves into the backs of their seats to let a man squeeze past them. 'I'm a doctor,' he muttered as he passed by. The woman was still limp; her head hung loosely with her mouth slightly open.

None of us knew what to do, so we just tried to focus on the stage, on Blanche/Blanchett's monologue down there. I was curious about the actors. Were they wondering if someone was dying up here, or if it was a terrorist attack, something real and human and far away?

It seemed like an eternity, but by the time paramedics had arrived and an oxygen mask had been put on the woman, the same scene was still playing onstage. The daughter slid out of the theatre with her mother and everything fell silent again, except for the performers. At intermission, as the lights came up, people in the audience turned to each other, talking about what happened. No one was talking about the play.

Mum and I pushed through the crowds filling the small foyer and lined up in the toilet queue. I had been looking forward to coming to see this show for a long time—we'd booked the tickets a year in advance. We were all dressed up and it was special to be in a new city with my friends and our mums. But now I felt uneasy. I waited in the queue for ages and tuned in to the hum of people now talking about their weeks, their days.

I heard fragments of dialogue, people's lives, how the babysitter was late, the husband had been ill, the boss was being annoying. Women still keeping their conversations going behind toilet cubicles, and politely holding the door open for each other when they left. As I was washing my hands I called out to my mum, asking if she was still inside, but she didn't reply. Obviously she was already outside, but hearing my own voice call out 'Mum' made me suddenly want to cry.

I went to Melbourne to visit. The acting study had bolstered me. I felt ready to confront my past. It was the first time I'd been back in two and a half years, since I'd left for New York. Every corner I turned there was some memory waiting for me, down alleyways at art openings, in bars and at tram stops. Everywhere, it seemed, something had happened to me in that city that now remained petrified in time, my Pompeii of memories, while life kept moving around it.

I'd left some clothes at Jack's when I'd left for New York so I dropped by to collect them. They were stored in a cheap candy-cane-striped bag in his warehouse, where he had set up a recording studio. He lived there with friends and they'd established a lively hub of creative energy, where artists, musicians and dancers congregated and thrived. When I saw it I was impressed—in the years I'd been away he'd been busy building up a flourishing artistic space that meant something to a lot of people.

Jack was doing really well. He was going on a tour of the US soon with a band he recorded. His first time overseas. He took me to a disused corner of the warehouse, pushing aside other garbage bags of junk and pulling out my clothes for me. Right there I unzipped the bags, thumbing through the dresses, stuff I'd worn years earlier. I was reunited with lots of old favourites, like the lace white Gatsby croquet dress I had found for six dollars and a crocheted, long seventies multi-coloured dress of Mum's. There was also the olive cardigan Reuben had given me years earlier and, digging even deeper, I found the shirt he was wearing the first time I met him, which I'd sentimentally salvaged when he was throwing it out. I tried to remember why it was important, what meaning it had once had for me, but it seemed so far away now. I threw it into the skip bin out the front.

I stayed over at Jack's that night, in the little partition off to the side that he had made into his bedroom. The mattress was on the floor. He pulled out the small suitcase his record player was sitting on and opened it to show me. Inside were all my letters, and photos of us. He'd kept them all. Letters I'd sent from Melbourne the year I'd arrived, when I'd told him about being in love with Reuben and I had discovered how terrible and wonderful life was, and our messages from the Killer Python letterbox. And postcards I'd sent him from New York, Thailand, India. As we sifted through them all I felt myself getting really sad. I felt silly, choked up with grief over what I'd thrown away and lost and what Jack had kept. He gave me a hug. 'Thank you for breaking up with me all those years ago,' he said, his voice unusually solemn. 'It was brave.'

I laughed in surprise. 'It felt like the opposite of brave,' I said. 'It felt weak, like I was running away from something instead of dealing with it.'

'Nah, we just both did the best we could at the time,' he said. Jack had always known the right thing to say to calm me down or cheer me up, but this was the kindest and most generous thing he'd ever said to me.

As we lay down next to each other to go to sleep, I could smell his dirty hair on the pillow beside me. I hadn't had sex with anyone in two years. It wasn't something I brooded about usually, just a realisation that hit me every now and then. It wasn't something I'd planned—I hadn't signed any chastity pledge—but it had just happened. Each day I thought it wouldn't last. But the longer it went on, I almost became proud of my record. I started to feel like I didn't want to break it, at least not for someone I didn't really like. The more I knew who I was, it became harder and harder to fall in love. I tried to remember what it felt like to be crazy, dippy, mad for someone. My fear was that I'd turned a corner and there was no going back to how it used to be, when there were always lovers around. I had tried to talk about my predicament to friends, but it was hard to articulate because I didn't understand it myself. If I started blaming myself for being ugly or unappealing to men, I turned almost immediately indignant and defensive; after all, I reasoned, it's not like I'd found any men who were so attractive or appealing either. Sex had always been something I'd fallen giddily into, simply and spontaneously, with whomever was nearest and most interesting. Now it had become a riddle I was trying to solve, like there was an equation to it or a scientific method of pairing up with the right person. But whenever I got caught up in worrying about it, my own self-pity annoyed me, so I forcibly brushed it aside. I had plenty of other things to do. I would want it when I wanted it, I told myself. I had no idea when that would be, whether this would continue for three years, or four, or five, but I tried not to think about that. Anyway, it really could change any day, any hour, any minute. I might meet someone.

Jack put his hands around my waist and pulled me closer towards him in his half-sleep. But he didn't do anything and neither did I. *Want something*, Stella Adler said, and it gave a character momentum, a direction to move in. The things you wanted were a path that showed you where to go. We both fell asleep until midday, no sun reaching us through the thick musty walls of the warehouse. I woke with him snuggled in close, spooning me, his arms still round my waist. I felt his hands on my hipbones, slippery over my nightie, hugging me. In the floaty sleepiness of waking up, he kissed me square on the mouth, but when we got up later neither of us mentioned it. Like a spell was broken.

The day before my audition, I went for a walk along the beach, practising my monologues. I muttered Cleopatra's lines, my gestures sometimes breaking out so that I must have looked like a crazy person to people walking past. It was low tide, and the beach was long and wide. The glassy violet corpses of bluebottles were sprinkled over the sand like discarded jelly shots; couples walked arm in arm, something serious and silent between them. It felt like I was the only one talking on the beach, and even I was mostly doing it in my head.

That night, my sister Xanthe dropped her daughter off to stay and she slept in the room next to mine. In the middle of the night I heard her crying. 'Poppy, what's wrong?' I went into the other room and turned on the bedside lamp. My little niece's face was hot from crying in the cool night, her eyes puffed up. When she saw a familiar face she became so hysterical she could hardly speak. She tried to breathe through her tears and her words came out all hiccupy. I tried to reassure her. 'It's okay, your mum and dad will come and get you in the morning. Everything's okay.'

She took a deep breath. 'I'm sorry,' she said in a tone a lot older than she was. 'I just get like this because I miss my mum.'

'Me too,' I told her, climbing into the single bed with her and wrapping her in my arms so we could fall asleep together. 'It's okay. I miss my mum whenever I'm away from her too.'

In the foyer of the Queensland Conservatory of Music, everyone was doing their eccentric warm-up prep. Some people were pacing, making soundless shapes with their lips, others were lying on the carpeted floor, eyes closed, others sat frozen on chairs, arms folded across their torsos. People looked away quickly when I made eye contact. By the time we'd filed into the big audition room I could count about sixty of us. I felt that anxious, familiar emotion again of being a lot older than any of these people. But maturity was good, I reminded myself. I thought back to *Bye Bye Birdie* and the ridiculous theatrics that I might have arrived here with if I'd come fresh from high school. Now I was older, wiser. I could be Cleopatra.

The directors of NIDA had flown up from Sydney, and in booming voices they began with a monologue of their own, explaining in detail how difficult the school was to get into and how many sacrifices we'd have to make if we got in. Then, at last, they clapped their hands and we got started.

One by one we were called up to do our audition pieces. When it was my turn I took a deep breath and pushed my shoulders as far back as I could. I unwrinkled my forehead and felt the skin on my face become a mask like I had practised. I walked to the centre of the room, turned to the audience and began.

Give me my robe, put on my crown. I have immortal longings in me!

I did the piece exactly as I'd practised it and as I spoke I noticed individual faces in the audience, bored, nervous, each person off in their own world, the stars of their own interior shows. I was aware of the concrete walls and the tall dome ceiling. The coldness of the floor I'd just been sitting on still clung to the backs of my thighs. I always thought I'd be transported during the magic of the dramatic moment, pulled out of my body onto some other plane, but I remained in the room of ordinary people and faces, with their stories that I had no clue about swirling around in their own minds. I tried to imagine where each of them had come from to get to this room: Who had cajoled them, what had driven them? Did they put as much preparation in as I had? Maybe more? Some of them were just winging it, you could tell. Others were so natural and charming, so obviously talented that it made me want to shrink into the floor.

When I sat down the room clapped politely the same way they did after everyone's performance.

I tried to feel proud of myself—after all, I had got through it, I'd done it, I hadn't messed up in any huge way, I had done fine—but everything was all tangled up with the uncomfortable feeling that this wasn't right. The sort of acting Stella had taught me wasn't about hiding yourself under the cover of a character; it was about revealing yourself, and in the discipline of that you became not just an actor but more yourself. I wanted to explore that every day, not just in a role I sometimes played on stage. Bringing everything I had learnt and felt and experienced to every new character is what excited me about acting. But did I really have to wait around for someone to give me a role?

Cleopatra wanted something. The directors of NIDA wanted something. Jack wanted something. And as I crossed my legs on the cold floor, I realised I wanted something too, and it wasn't this. I didn't have the drive to become an actor. As auditions continued in the centre of the room, I felt a weight lightening, a pressure lifting. I thought about what else I didn't want. I didn't want to be living in Buderim. Or to keep moving back home with my parents. I didn't want to reach for something that wasn't me anymore. I didn't want to play a character.

I wanted a certain emotion, or rather, lots of them. Delight, despair, hope and hurt.

And that happened whenever I put on my dresses. When I hit upon the perfect feeling, and I went through my day wearing it, no matter what else happened I experienced that feeling for that time. And it was right.

I had my dresses. Everyone seems to think fashion is what other people are wearing—it's a thing you do for other people, that it's how they see you, but for me it has always been how I see myself.

I thought about all the parts I had played over the years. The ordinary events made special because I was aware of what was happening, because I was fully alive in my body and my dress, because I was fully inhabiting the role I'd decided to play that day, the fun of it; the joy of bringing to your everyday life magic and imagination and artistry and interest was a gift. It was an ordinary gift anyone could have. Why was I searching for a feeling on stage when I could get it any day?

The NIDA directors asked just five people to stay back to continue auditioning. Everyone else was told thank you. I drove home with a dizzying sense of freedom, of being released at last. It was over.

When I got home I opened my computer and there was an email from an editor at *The Age* newspaper in Melbourne. She told me she had seen some of my writing, and asked me if I wanted to try writing a column for them. It was one of those unexpected, amazing opportunities that appears at just the right time. It was another audition, but this one I had been preparing for for a decade. A week later I'd got the job: a weekly column at a newspaper. I was going to have a regular income; I would be writing full-time for a living. At last, I *wanted* something.

When I said goodbye at the airport, my mum looked smaller than usual. The hugs had become too big now and I towered over her. I had lived away for so long but every time I left I still missed my parents. I got childishly nostalgic for curling up with them, chuckling as we all watched TV, my gangly legs thrown across both of them and Mum's arms hugging my ankles like a fishtail skirt the moment before it splits in two, Dad's after-dinner instant-coffee breath floating near by.

Melbourne was the least faraway place I'd moved to in years, but right now it felt the furthest.

I kissed my parents and said goodbye.

I was going to turn thirty there. It felt momentous. I bought a brand-new vintage dress for my birthday with the first paycheck I'd had in ages. A dress full of hope, to hold new memories in. Shiny fabric that shimmers when it's hit with light. Puffy shoulders. Bold and strong, the colour of a bruised grape—the sort of hue a younger woman mightn't be able to pull off so easily but now I could carry it. A mix of 1940s and 1980s, Joan Crawford crossed with Joan Collins.

I invited all my friends and we sat in a beautiful backyard and ate dinner under dripping ornamental grapevines, tea-light candles and glowing white flowers placed in jars on every flat surface. Friends new and old, some with partners and some without, some with careers they loved and others who would continue searching for the things that brought meaning to every day. Some who would go on to have children together and others who would break up. Looking around at the people in my life I could see that the possibilities for where you were meant to go next were open, the choices were your own.

I'm exactly like everyone else, I realised happily, and as I moved to get up I could feel the dress press against my skin, and my body, warm and alive, holding all my memories inside.

Acknowledgements

To everyone who appears in these stories, thank you and I'm sorry.

Thanks to the team at Allen & Unwin for all their support, especially to Foong Ling Kong, without whom this book wouldn't exist. Thank you also to my editor Kathryn Knight, and to Claire Kingston, Louise Cornege, Caitlin Withey, Marie Slocombe, Jo Lyons and Katie Evans, and to Allison Colpoys for her exquisite cover design.

Sofija Stefanovic, my first reader, has offered the most helpful and encouraging advice throughout and I couldn't have done it without her. Anna Krien, Ruby Murray and Benjamin Law all read later drafts of the manuscript and gave invaluable editorial assistance and support. Marieke Hardy was an early champion of my writing and is the sole owner of a homemade 'I Heart Young Professionals' T-shirt. I can't thank all you guys enough.

My eternal gratitude to Jo Duck for the photographs, and to Sarah Lea Cross and Nataley Tourmey for hair and make-up. Thanks also to Jeremy Valentine and Grant Franci at Shag (www.shagshop.com.au) who generously loaned us accessories for the shoot.

I'm extremely grateful to Lee Sandwith, Noella Thomson, Ruby Murray, Dane Ash, Sarah Trotter, Pete Garrow, Ronnie Scott, Alice Swing and Lachlan Waite, and everyone else who donated time, props and wise counsel to help make the blog *dressmemory. com* what it is.

Thanks to all the readers and audiences at the Women of Letters shows—being among you every month fills me up and drives me forward. And especially to Michaela McGuire, Liam Pieper and Marieke for letting me be a part of it, and for their continued support. A small section of the chapter 'Twenty-eight' was read out in a slightly different form at one of those shows and published as 'A Letter to the History I'd Like to Rewrite' in *Yours Truly* (Penguin, 2013).

Special thanks to Romy Ash, Anna Barnes, Gabi Barton, Ali Bird, Hannah Brooks, Rhianna Boyle, Clare Chippendale, Caro Cooper, Kate Cooper, Chimere Cisse, Tom Doig, Ady Downie, Jack Farley, Claire Feain, Amy Gillies, Stuart Glover, Natalie Gregg, Phoebe Gregg, Pete Goodwin, Candice Hill, Megan Reeder Hope, Ross Hope, Niki Horin, Gill Hutchison, Tait Ischia, Krystyna Kobylinski, Burcu Koray, Michelle Law, Mark Limmage, Nikki Lusk, Johnny Mackay, Jess McGuire, Laura Jean McKay, William Mills, Simone Mitchell, Nadia Mizner, Blythe Moore, Beck Newham, Andrea Parkyn, Ian Rogers, Miriam Rosenbloom, Luke Ryan, Kate Scott, Scott Spark, Natalija Stefanovic, Estelle Tang,

Gill Tucker, Amy Vuleta, Sarah Wallace and Emily York. Thanks also to Copperfields Restaurant in Olinda, Victoria, and to my friends at The Improv Conspiracy, who taught me to be less afraid of the blank white page.

Thank you so much to Grace Lee for illustrating the story of the 'making of the book' *Nobody Is Making You Do This*, which can be viewed online. And to Que Minh, Eliza Sarlos and Gabriel Clarke for including it in their Graphic Festival program.

To my parents, Lyn and Geoff, who are the best. And to Xanthe, Analiese, Lachy, Terese, Sam, Michael, Ayla, Oscar, Henry and Poppy. I love you guys.

Lastly, to Jeremy, Levi and Winifred. I can't decide if you're an epilogue to this book or a prologue to another one—both, I reckon.